Ancient
Mysteries
of Britain

Ancient Mysteries of Britain

Janet and Colin Bord

DIAMOND ◆ BOOKS

First published in 1986 by Grafton Books,
a division of HarperCollins*Publishers* Ltd.

Copyright © Janet and Colin Bord 1986

This edition published in 1991 by Diamond Books,
a division of HarperCollins*Publishers* Ltd.

British Library Cataloguing in Publication Data

Bord, Janet
    Ancient Mysteries of Britain.
    1. Mythology, British   2. Great Britain—
    Antiquities
    I. Title   II. Bord, Colin
    936.1   DA90

ISBN 0 583 31311 6

Typeset by Ace Filmsetting Ltd, Frome, Somerset
Printed in Hong Kong

Contents

Preface

Thirteen years ago we wrote a book called *Mysterious Britain* which gave a taste of Britain and Ireland's rich past, with examples of the many surviving relics of ancient history. Since writing our first book we have travelled widely and have discovered many more mysterious and wonderful places, so we felt the time was right to produce another book continuing the story we began in 1972. In *Ancient Mysteries of Britain* we give details of many more places to visit as well as fresh thoughts on some of the major sites already covered in *Mysterious Britain* so that you too can enjoy at first hand the ancient mysteries of Britain and Ireland.

The remains of prehistoric man's homes, tombs and temples, earthworks, rock carvings, early Christian crosses, caves, Roman ruins, early churches, hill-figures, holy wells, the Arthurian legend, dragons, mazes, folklore, customs and traditions, leys and earth energies, and finally some twentieth-century mysteries – all these are represented in this book, and we include a small selection of the best examples in the 'Places to Visit' at the end of each chapter. Location details are given for all the sites included in Places to Visit, followed by the Ordnance Survey map reference. Other sites will be found in the guidebooks listed in the Bibliography, where are also listed books which describe certain aspects of our subject-matter in much greater detail. Most of the books mentioned have appeared within the last fifteen years, many within the last five, and therefore they should still be fairly easily available, in libraries if not still in print.

Most of the photographs are our own, but we have used several supplied by our friends Hamish Brown (pp. 48, 51, 54, 74, 110, 164), Margaret Ponting (p. 13) and Anthony Weir (pp. 31, 39, 46, 62, 79, 83 [both], 84, 87, 99, 119, 137, 142); and a few other sources, as follows: BBC Hulton Picture Library, pp. 220, 232; Fortean Picture Library, pp. 193, 196, 239, 247, 251, 257; University of Cambridge Committee for Aerial Photography, pp. 147, 153.

*Ancient
Mysteries
of Britain*

1. *Stone circles: astronomical observatories?*

The visible relics of prehistoric Britain and Ireland pose questions which can only be tentatively answered, since they are at least 2,000 years old and some are as much as 5,000 years old. Perhaps the most enigmatic are the stone circles, more than 900 of which have been identified in Britain, mostly in the upland areas. Many of these circles have been damaged with only a few random stones now remaining, but a few major sites have survived centuries of indifference, to become centres of controversy in the late twentieth century.

Archaeological investigation has shown that stone circles were being built for 1,800 years, between 3000 and 1200 BC, but except for a few sites where items have been found buried, there is nothing for archaeologists to study other than the layout of the stones and their location. This approach was followed by Professor Alexander Thom, who over several decades surveyed hundreds of stone circles in an attempt to decipher their meaning. He found that not all the circles were in fact circular. Many were laid out as egg shapes, ellipses, or flattened circles, all seeming to show incredible geometrical precision long before the age of Pythagoras. He also identified a standard unit of measurement, 2.722 feet, which he called the megalithic yard. It seemed to Professor Thom that the purpose of all this was to enable the scientists of the time to precisely observe the movements of the sun and moon, and especially to be able to predict lunar eclipses. How they could have achieved this without scientific instruments such as are used today is an involved study, and anyone wishing to explore this further is advised to obtain Thom's three books, *Megalithic Sites in Britain* (1967), *Megalithic Lunar Observatories* (1971) and *Megalithic Remains in Britain and Brittany* (1978), though a good understanding of geometry will be required by the reader. Stated simply, the method thought to have been employed was to align individual stones in a circle with markers in the surrounding landscape, either artificially erected standing stones, or prominent natural features such as hills and mountains. Professor Thom was often able to identify the markers which he believed had been used in this way. Other types of sites, such as burial chambers and lines of standing stones, were also thought to have been used for astronomical purposes.

When read in detail, Professor Thom's evidence for the precise construction and use of stone circles and other sites may seem conclusive. But recently some doubts have been raised, regarding the precision of the circles' construction, and the precision of the observations for which they could have been used. One researcher has shown that a detailed knowledge of geometry was not needed to lay out the stones: it could have been done using pegs and ropes. Also, the megalithic yard does not appear to have been commonly used throughout Britain, but principally in Scotland. Archaeologists also have some doubts about the feasibility of using sites in the way Professor Thom has suggested: Are the long-distance sight lines realistic, or do they only serve to support Thom's theories? All unbiased researchers in whatever field should realise the dangers of holding a specific theory too rigidly – the evidence they note will tend to support their theory because the researchers unconsciously seek out the positive evidence and ignore the rest. Whether these doubts are appropriate in the case of Professor Thom's research and theories is difficult for the layman to decide, and no doubt the controversy over the amount of astronomical use to which stone circles and other sites were put will continue. However, it would appear that many circles did have some function of this kind, though perhaps of a less precise nature than originally envisaged. Instead of an elite group of scientist–astronomers, able to exert control over the common people by their supposedly magical ability to predict eclipses and other dramatic heavenly events, a more reasonable scenario is now suggested, showing the circles in use as meeting places where ceremonies and rituals were performed, at specific times as plotted by simple astronomical observations.

Lacking any written records from these distant times (though see Chapter 6, which describes what may be written records, if only they could be deciphered), there is little to suggest what kinds of ceremonials were performed. We have only hints of our ancestors' way of life, from artefacts discovered in burial chambers, from folklore possibly handed down over several thousand years, and from the activities of similar peoples in other parts of the world, for example the American Indians, some of whom still perform ancient dances and rituals.

Stone circles: astronomical observatories?

It seems very likely that in Britain our ancestors behaved in a similar way. Their preoccupations would certainly have been the same – the promotion of fertility in the earth and its creatures, the promotion of favourable weather, and the worship of those elements (or 'gods') which seemed to control their lives. Perhaps some of the traditional customs described in Chapter 18 provide a direct link with rituals performed by prehistoric man in stone circles 4,000 years ago.

Although many stone circles were small, some were more elaborate and included enigmatic features. For example, among the 'Places to Visit' at the end of this chapter is Boscawen-Un (Cornwall), a circle with a large standing stone at its centre. This stone is now leaning, and may have been erected at this angle. What was its significance? Long Meg and Her Daughters (Cumbria) is another site where a standing stone (Long Meg) accompanies a circle (Her Daughters), though in this instance the stone stands outside the circle. Castlerigg circle (Cumbria) contains a rectangle formed of ten stones, while Callanish (Lewis/Western Isles) has a circle to which lead several rows of standing stones, forming a rough cross with the circle at its centre. The Hurlers (Cornwall) consists of three circles of differing sizes standing in a line, while Stanton Drew (Avon) also has three circles, one of them being much larger than the others, almost 400 feet across and the second largest

Callanish standing stones (Lewis/Western Isles) at midsummer sunrise, one of the significant events of the year watched for by prehistoric man at his astronomical observatories.

circle in Britain. The so-called 'recumbent stone circles' of north-east Scotland, about eighty of them, each have a large stone lying on its side at the southern edge of the circle. These features, and others not mentioned here, may possibly have had an astronomical significance, but it is extremely difficult to be certain, and it is only through detailed research by archaeologists and others that anything at all is known about these sites.

The amount of time and effort which can be expended on a site, both by its builders and by archaeologists researching into it, is best illustrated by Stonehenge, which is certainly the most famous prehistoric site in Britain, and possibly in the world, attracting millions of visitors annually. Despite all the attention that has been paid to Stonehenge, by archaeologists and others with relevant specialist knowledge, its mysteries are still only partially revealed to us, for it is a most complex site which has undergone several phases of construction. It is an example of a henge, differing from the stone circles we have described earlier in being a circular enclosure formed by banks and ditches, inside which may be one or more circles of stones (as at Avebury, Stonehenge, and Arbor Low), or a circle of wooden posts, long since decayed, or shafts containing bones and tools, or large wooden buildings, or nothing at all. There are more than seventy henges known in Britain, and they were built during 1,000 years from the late Neolithic into the Early Bronze Age, roughly in the middle of the period when stone circles were being built. They are thought to have been places where the people gathered together, for domestic events like fairs, or for religious ceremonies, or perhaps for both. Certainly a tremendous amount of effort was expended in constructing these henges, so they were clearly of great importance. Deep ditches were dug, and in the case of Stonehenge, massive stones were somehow transported great distances, eighty of them, the 'bluestones', being brought by sea from the Prescelly Mountains in west Wales. They weighed around 4 tons each, but seem small beside the impressive sarsen stones which average 26 tons in weight. These were brought from north Wiltshire, not such a great distance as the bluestones but nevertheless quite a feat of transportation. Whether all this was done in order to construct an observatory, capable of many complex astronomical calculations, as some of today's computer-addicted scientists would like to think, is still open to conjecture. It may have been simply to build an impressive structure where important rituals could be performed, its role as an observatory being less important and less precise than was once thought.

which the stones were put. They have always held a strong fascination. In earlier centuries, people even used to chip pieces off The King Stone for good luck charms, especially soldiers going into battle. The witchcraft connection has extended to the present day, with rumours of modern witches using the stone circle secretly at night to perform their rituals. Rollright has also been the focus in recent years of intensive scientific research into earth energies and the possible role of stone circles and standing stones in harnessing and channelling such energies. More details of this research, known as the Dragon Project, are given in Chapter 19.

Torhouse stone circle, Wigtown/Dumfries & Galloway Region

Location: 3½ miles west of Wigtown, and beside the B733. (NX 382565)

Nineteen boulders of local granite, now lichen-covered, form a small circle standing on a manmade platform of earth and stones. There is also a stone standing between two larger ones,

Torhouse stone circle.

somewhat reminiscent of the recumbent stone circles of north-east Scotland. Since at least the seventeenth century, this site was believed to be the burial place of a mythical king, Galdus.

Arbor Low henge, Derbyshire

Location: 4½ miles south-west of Bakewell, just east of the A515 and reached along a farm track. (SK 160636)

This henge is located at an impressive upland site with distant views, and its circle of prostrate stones makes it unique. No one is sure whether the stones ever stood upright. No evidence of holes has been found, so perhaps the stones were in very shallow holes or were only propped up. Traces of a burial were found near the central group of stones, and during excavations at the beginning of this century an antler pick was found, also thirteen ox-teeth, six flint flakes and scrapers in new condition and therefore deliberately buried, and an arrowhead. Burials were also found in the barrow which was built at a later date into the outer bank, and in another nearby barrow known as Gib Hill. A low bank of earth leads from the henge towards and past Gib Hill, possibly leading to what may have been an earlier henge.

Loanhead of Daviot recumbent stone circle, Aberdeen/Grampian Region

Location: 5 miles north-west of Inverurie, and just off a lane to the north of Daviot. (NJ 748289)

Considerable archaeological attention has been paid to this circle, in 1934 and more recently in the 1970s by Aubrey Burl. It was built around 2500 BC and is a classic example of a recumbent stone circle of which there are about eighty, all in north-east Scotland. They are small circles, probably built by single families with neighbours helping to move the large recumbent stone. The consistent placing of this stone at the south side of the circle is puzzling, one possible explanation being that the full moon at midsummer could appear to travel along the recumbent stone, the effect being especially dramatic every few years when it came closer to the horizon and may have appeared to enter the gateway formed by the tall pillars and recumbent stone. Inside the circle are small stones which may be the remains of a cairn, either contemporary with the circle or added later. Several small cairns were found beside the stand-

ing stones, one of them containing a small cup possibly used to hold incense. Pottery from later ages suggests that the site was reused, the central cairn perhaps serving as a dwelling, since a small hearth was found inside it.

Drombohilly Upper stone circle, County Kerry

Location: 1½ miles north-east of Lauragh Bridge and just to the east of a byroad. (V 79 61)

There are over 180 stone circles in Ireland, the most impressive of them being in Cork and Kerry. These southern circles are known as axial-stone circles because usually at the south-west is a stone lying lengthwise opposite two stones called portals, thus defining the circle's axis of orientation. Unfortunately the axial stone is missing at Drombohilly Upper, as is one other stone of the probable eleven that formed the circle. A stone-built rectangular mound close by may have been connected with the circle. This circle's siting on a knoll giving magnificent views over the surrounding countryside follows a pattern we have already noted, that many circles are found in open and prominent positions. Why this should be is not clear, but it does suggest a link of some kind with the surrounding landscape

22

features, possibly astronomical, possibly as an echo of the content of the rituals performed, which may have been intended to promote the fertility of the land and to invoke protection against threats both natural and manmade.

The Hurlers stone circles, Cornwall

Location: On Bodmin Moor, 4 miles north of Liskeard and close to the village of Minions. (SX 258713)

Three separate circles make up The Hurlers, the largest being 135 feet across. The name refers to the old game of hurling, the stones being men turned to stone for playing the game on a Sunday. Some of the stones were shaped, and those of the central circle were erected so that their tops were level. The northern circle had been paved with granite, hints of a ritual usage of this site. Professor Thom identified several astronomical alignments, but it is thought by some researchers to be impossible to assess the validity of the alignments here and at other sites, in view of the changing positions of the heavenly bodies over the centuries, coupled with the necessarily imprecise dating of the circles.

'A redoubled numbering never eveneth with the first ... But far stranger is the country people's report that once they were men, and for their hurling upon the Sabbath, so metamorphosed.' Thus did Richard Carew in his Survey of Cornwall *(1602) describe two aspects of The Hurlers' folklore: that the stones cannot be counted, and that they are men turned to stone.*

Callanish standing stones, Isle of Lewis/Western Isles

Location: At Callanish village, 13 miles west of Stornoway. (NB 214331)

Astronomical observatory, calendrical computer, ceremonial site ... Callanish has been seen as all these, and more. Its unique layout makes it especially difficult to interpret. There is a small circle of tall stones with a 275-foot avenue of stones leading to it from the south-west. There are also three shorter single rows of stones (avenues never completed) leading off the circle, the whole forming a cross-shape with the circle at the crossing-point. There are also the remains of a burial chamber within the circle, this probably having been added later, as has happened elsewhere. Over the centuries the beliefs of the people changed, and the earlier monuments lost their significance or were adapted to suit changing needs, as at Stonehenge. If a monument were to be rebuilt, the old site was often retained, because although ideas changed, the sites were still considered potent. At Bryn-Celli-Ddu on Anglesey (see Chapter 2) a large tomb was built over an earlier henge, almost completely obliterating it. At Callanish the stones had a very strong hold over the people, keeping their reputation as a sacred site long after the builders had been forgotten, and this aura of sanctity preserved the site from destruction.

Legends give hints of ceremonial use, and during this century several researchers have suggested astronomical alignments, so there is a strong possibility that Callanish was active in a similar way to the other sites we have already described. Aubrey Burl in his *The Stone Circles of the British Isles* draws our attention to the fact that the long stone avenue leads downhill towards the bay, thus providing a link between the stone circle and a water source. Callanish is by no means the only place where this connection has been observed, and there is a strong possibility that part of the ritual practices involved water. Water-cults were an important part of prehistoric and Celtic religious practices, and have even survived to the present day, a subject we discuss more fully in our book *Sacred Waters*.

Stonehenge, Wiltshire

Location: 10 miles north of Salisbury, and 2 miles west of Amesbury, on the A344. Access is restricted. (SU 123422)

There can be few people who have not heard of Stonehenge, and judging by the vast number of visitors each year, most people have been there too. With all the restrictive fences and guards, and the milling crowds (unless you can visit in bad winter weather), you may not find it easy to sense the power of this place. But the power does miraculously survive, despite the fortifications, and despite the ballyhoo at midsummer, when the Stonehenge Free Festival across the road is in full swing, and when the modern Druids come to perform their spurious ceremony. Those who visited Stonehenge before the 1950s will retain the best memories of it, for then it stood nearly deserted in elemental grandeur on Salisbury Plain, and few visitors came. As we write there are plans afoot to completely redesign the whole Stonehenge complex, including diverting the A344 and opening a new museum and information centre nearly a mile away, so that visitors will be able to walk across the downs to Stonehenge via other prehistoric sites. This scheme is to be welcomed, as it should improve the appearance and atmosphere of the area, as well as reducing the numbers of people actually at Stonehenge – only those seriously interested in seeing it will be bothered to walk there.

Stonehenge has had more attention paid to it by archaeologists than almost any other site, but it still retains its mysteries. Earlier generations than our own thought it was a Druid tem-

Geoffrey of Monmouth, twelfth-century chronicler, referred to Stonehenge as 'Giants' Dance', which may refer to an earlier belief that the stones were once giants. Another belief was that the monument was set up by Merlin, the magician of the King Arthur legends. The photograph shows a good example of a trilithon on the left, with others in the distance; and in the centre middle distance one of the bluestones, an upright and leaning pillar dwarfed by the huge trilithons. The 'knob' on top of the tall right-hand stone is a tenon carved to fit into a corresponding hole or mortise on the underside of a now fallen lintel stone, to hold it in place.

ple, but it is now known that Stonehenge was in existence 2,000 years before the Druids were active, and was probably in ruins during their time. Little is known about the real Druids, but they were believed to have conducted their rituals within groves of trees, and their only constructions were of wood, not stone. But the lurid picture of Stonehenge as a centre of Druid ritual and sacrifice was difficult to eradicate, and even today the misapprehension continues, fuelled by the modern Druids whose history dates back only to their foundation in 1833.

In the twentieth century Stonehenge has emerged as an astronomical observatory, following the computer-aided researches of Professor Gerald Hawkins in the 1960s. More recent discoveries have pointed up the existence of errors in the supposed alignments of certain stones with astronomical events, which has led to a reassessment of Stonehenge's role as an observatory. Some researchers have concluded that although Stonehenge may have been used in this way, the observations were not precise but only approximate, the intention being not to carry out scientific research as we understand it, but to follow the movements of the sky gods.

It is impossible to know whether the final use to which Stonehenge was put was the same as the use for which it was originally built, for it is clear that the monument underwent big changes throughout its approximately 1,500 years of active life. It was begun around 2800 BC, and the first Stonehenge consisted of a bank and ditch, a ring of fifty-six pits, and the so-called Heel Stone, the first stone to be erected. By 2100 BC, the eighty bluestones had been brought from Wales and erected in two concentric circles, but they were soon dismantled and the great sarsen stones were set up, some of the bluestones being reused inside the horseshoe of sarsens. By about 1800 BC the final Stonehenge was completed, the bluestones having again been dismantled and repositioned as they stand today.

People are now so distanced in time from the builders of Stonehenge that they find it difficult if not impossible to understand them and to appreciate what Stonehenge meant to them. Were some of the sarsens erected as trilithons (two uprights with a lintel carefully fitted across the top) simply to look impressive, or did this arrangement have some significance which eludes us? Why was it necessary to fetch eighty 4-ton stones from Wales? There are many more unanswered questions surrounding Stonehenge; if the builders of the final phase intended to leave behind them a monument to astound and mystify future generations, they have certainly succeeded.

2. *The house of the dead*

There is evidence of human burial in the earliest prehistoric times, the Old and Middle Stone Ages, but the first tombs date from the New Stone Age, after 4000 BC. These tombs are the oldest prehistoric monuments to survive in Britain. It has been suggested that the design for burial structures was derived from house designs, and even that some round barrows might have been built over the remains of circular huts. There is no doubt that great care was taken in housing the dead, and that over the centuries many thousands of tombs, some very elaborate, were constructed in Britain and Ireland.

The form they take varies according to the area where they were built, and the time when they were built. The most impressive to visit today are the chambered barrows and chambered cairns, mounds of earth or stones containing a burial chamber made of large stones. It is quite an experience to enter one of these with its roof in place – such as West Kennet long barrow (Wiltshire), or Stoney Littleton long barrow (Avon), or Bryn-Celli-Ddu (Anglesey), and there are a number of others not included in our 'Places to Visit' such as Maes Howe (Orkney), The Grey Cairns of Camster (Caithness), Hetty Pegler's Tump (Gloucestershire), and the passage-tombs in the prehistoric cemetery at the Bend of the Boyne (County Meath) which in addition to the famous Newgrange contains at least twenty-five tombs of this kind.

Sometimes the roof is missing and the stone passage is open to the sky, as at Capel Garmon (Gwynedd); sometimes the surrounding mound of earth has disappeared leaving a dramatic dolmen or cromlech, massive upright stones supporting a capstone so big and heavy that it is difficult to comprehend how it was ever raised up there. The capstone of Lligwy cromlech (Anglesey) weighs about 28 tons. But not all the stone tombs are well preserved. All that remains in many cases is a pile of tumbled stones, meaning nothing to the layman and only revealing something of its history to the archaeologist after long and careful examination. Most commonly seen are the grassy mounds called round barrows or tumuli, and the piles of small stones called cairns. They were built later than the bigger tombs and did not usually contain a separate stone burial chamber, though they might contain a stone box or cist. There are thought to be between 30,000 and 40,000 tumuli and cairns still surviving.

Even though many tombs have been robbed of their contents in previous centuries, archaeologists have recovered much in the way of skeletons and 'grave-goods', and these finds have added considerably to our knowledge of life in the Neolithic/ New Stone Age (when long barrows were built) and the Bronze Age (when round barrows were built). In the earlier tombs, flint implements were found, beads of bone, shell and stone, and pottery beakers, whereas in the later Bronze Age barrows

Although the tomb is now reduced to a few scattered boulders, Maen Pebyll near Nebo (Gwynedd) shows the typical open upland situation with fine vistas chosen by prehistoric tomb-builders.

the finds were richer – bronze daggers, axe-hammers and other masculine items of fine quality.

Although the emphasis so far has been on burial, it would be wrong to think that when the chief of a tribe died (for these elaborate tombs were surely only constructed for the aristocracy of the time), the workmen raised up a huge tomb, the corpse was buried with some personal belongings, and then the tomb was closed and left untouched for ever afterwards. There is clear evidence that the older tombs were in use for long periods of time. West Kennet long barrow, for instance, was used for around 1,000 years, many people being buried there at different times. We can compare such tombs to our own churches and cathedrals, which contain burials of many ages but are also used for other purposes. Rituals and ceremonies were doubtless performed at the tombs, some intended to assist the departing spirit on its journey into the next world and possibly some to commemorate and aid those who had died in earlier times, perhaps in battle.

Although there are no written records telling us what our ancestors thought about death, and whether they believed in an afterlife, there are some tantalising hints that they did not accept death as final. In some Neolithic chambered tombs bowls have been found which may have contained food offerings, while vessels found in Bronze Age barrows did originally contain food, as some remains of it were found, including animal bones. Apart from such practical considerations as providing the dead with food and drink, there is also some evidence that prehistoric men believed that the pattern of life, death and rebirth was linked to the rhythms of the sun and moon, which brings us back to the possible use of stone circles as astronomical observatories which we discussed in the previous chapter. As will be seen in Chapter 18, where traditional customs are described, midwinter is the time of death followed by rebirth and renewal, and this belief in the natural cycle stretches back in time, at least to the Neolithic tomb-builders and probably long before them. The builders of Newgrange, which is the most impressive chambered tomb in Europe, incorporated their beliefs into this monument. Some of them are in the form of carvings which cannot yet be positively interpreted, but there is one construction of unmistakable purpose. Above the entrance an aperture was made between two stone slabs, and just after sunrise at the winter solstice (21 December), and at no other time, a beam of sunlight shines through the aperture and down the passageway of the tomb. The light reaches to the burial chamber at the far end of the long passage, about 80 feet in all, and touches the edge of a basin, which once probably contained the cremated remains of the dead. This event lasts for around fifteen minutes, and then as the earth turns the sun leaves the inner tomb which remains in darkness for another twelve months.

That this strange and eerie happening is unlikely to be a result of chance is shown by the fact that at Maes Howe tomb (Orkney) a similar aperture has been found at the entrance to the passage. Maes Howe was built about 500 years later than Newgrange, around 2500 BC. The construction of only a small aperture to allow the sun to enter suggests that this was intended as a private event, to be experienced by the dead alone, and just as the midwinter sun marked the return of vitality to all forms of life, so its entry into these tombs could have symbolised the continuance of life for those who had died. Symbols probably meant to represent the sun were carved on a stone on the outside of the passage grave at Dowth, near Newgrange, but the many other carvings at burial sites, especially in Ireland, are not so easy of interpretation (see Chapter 6). It is likely that if only they could be read, they would have much to tell us about life and death as seen through the eyes of prehistoric man.

PLACES TO VISIT

Newgrange passage-tomb, County Meath

Location: 3 miles south-east of Slane; signposted. (O 00 72)

Newgrange is the most famous and impressive of the passage-tombs in the barrow cemetery at the Bend of the Boyne. It has been restored, some say unsympathetically, and in becoming a tourist attraction it has lost much of its atmosphere. But it still remains impressive, especially the many carvings, both inside and out. The tomb consists of a large mound about 250 feet in diameter and originally 50 feet high. All around the edge stand ninety-seven kerbstones, many elaborately decorated, the entrance stone (illustrated here) being one of the most beautiful. Its spiral motif is repeated in other carvings inside the tomb. Behind the entrance stone a passage 60 feet long leads to three

The beautifully carved stone at the entrance to Newgrange passage-tomb.

small chambers containing massive stone basins, which presumably held offerings or burials or both. Carvings of spirals, lozenges, chevrons, triangles and meanders decorate a number of the stone slabs in the passage, the chambers and the corbelled roof (the famous triple spiral is illustrated in Chapter 6).

Other tombs in the Boyne Cemetery worth visiting include Dowth and Knowth. Dowth is one of the earliest passage-tombs in Ireland, and like Newgrange there are decorated stones, but not so impressive. There are three passages at Dowth, two leading into tombs and the third into a souterrain (see Chapter 9 for an explanation of this term) which was added much later. At Knowth the carvings rival those at Newgrange and are again found inside and outside the tomb. The large mound contains two passage-graves (the passages, over 100 feet long, are the longest in any tomb in Europe) and several souterrains, and fifteen or sixteen 'satellite' passage-graves stand around the tomb. The Bend of the Boyne is truly an amazing place to visit!

West Kennet long barrow, Wiltshire

Location: South of Avebury and not far from Silbury Hill, signposted off the A4. (SU 104677)

West Kennet lies on the crest of a hill with a fine view across fields to Silbury Hill and Avebury beyond. The barrow is more than 320 feet long and 8 feet high, the actual stone passage running only 33 feet into the mound at its eastern end. There are five small chambers inside, two either side and one at the end of the passage, all of which were found to contain burials when excavated. Forty-six burials have been found, and there is evidence that many more remains were removed in the seventeenth century, some of them by Dr Toope of Marlborough who used the bones to make medicines. Also found were flints, beads, animal bones and pottery, the dating of which indicates that the tomb was in use for about 1,000 years. At the end of this period, the tomb was filled up with chalk rubble, the entrance forecourt was filled with boulders, and three large slabs were used to seal it all off. These are still in place, but the interior has been cleared out and restored, and can be entered.

Although the tomb layout described here is the one usually found, a few tombs had 'false entrances', such as the long barrow known as Belas Knap (Gloucestershire). The impressive entrance leads nowhere; the stone-built burial chambers

were dug into the sides of the 175-foot mound. This is likely to have been done to mislead would-be tomb robbers. Another example is Capel Garmon chambered long barrow (Gwynedd), described elsewhere in this chapter.

The entrance to West Kennet long barrow was sealed off with huge slabs of stone, but a new way in has been made to allow access.

Cairnholy chambered cairns, Kirkcudbright/ Dumfries & Galloway Region

Location: Reached via a lane leading north off the A75 between Gatehouse of Fleet and Newton Stewart, just over a mile west of the Auchenlarie Holiday Farm caravan park. (NX 517538)

Two cairns stand near each other at an upland site overlooking the sea. Cairnholy I, the first to be reached along the lane, is the most impressive. Behind a façade of tall stones are the ruins of a burial chamber in a low mound nearly 170 feet long. The site was excavated in 1949 and traces of fires were found on the ground in front of the entrance. These had been lit while the tomb was in use, and may have been the fires in which the dead were cremated before being placed in the tomb. The tomb was blocked by stones when it went out of use in the Early Bronze Age, but another burial was placed in the chamber in the Middle Bronze Age, accompanied by a cup and ring marked stone.

33

Cairnholy I.

The original layout of Cairnholy II is less easy to see as the tomb is more ruinous; and the 1949 excavators discovered that the contents of the burial chamber had already been removed. They found only a knife, scraper, arrowhead, and pottery sherds of both Neolithic and Early Bronze Age date.

The name 'Cairnholy' may derive from Carn Ulaidh, the treasure cairn; such places were often thought to conceal hoards of treasure, but the local people were often afraid to put these beliefs to the test, for fear of retribution.

Bryn-Celli-Ddu chambered cairn, Anglesey, Gwynedd

Location: About 4 miles south-west of Menai Bridge, reached along a farm track near Llandaniel Fab. (SH 508702)

There are several intriguing features at this burial site, the first being its location directly on top of a former henge. Also intriguing are the suggestions of rituals performed here: the small three-sided structure outside the entrance where an ox had been sacrificed; and the pit in the centre of the mound, behind the burial chamber, where a burnt human ear-bone was found. The carved stone now standing in the pit is a replica of a stone which was found lying nearby, the original being in the National Museum of Wales. It carries a strange meander

34

design, possibly symbolising the journey of the soul, or acting as a protection for the soul on its journey. The burial chamber itself is no less interesting, being constructed of very large slabs of stone. The 27-foot passage contains a low stone bench where offerings may have been left, and inside the chamber is an enigmatic 4-foot standing stone, smooth and rounded. Fragments of bone, burnt and unburnt, were found inside the tomb.

'Bryn-Celli-Ddu' means 'the hill in the dark grove', which hints of the Druids, who worshipped in groves of trees and whose last stronghold was this island of Anglesey. Perhaps the spirits once believed to live at Bryn-Celli-Ddu were the spirits of those last Druids, who died cruelly at the hands of the Romans.

The entrance to Bryn-Celli-Ddu chambered cairn; the stone kerb was positioned in the ditch of the former henge.

Pentre Ifan cromlech, Dyfed

Location: 7 miles south-west of Cardigan, hidden down a network of lanes but well signposted. (SN 099370)

Pentre Ifan is one of the best examples of a cromlech or dolmen, a Neolithic burial chamber whose covering mound of earth has long since been eroded and dispersed. Traces show the mound to have been about 130 feet long. The delicately poised capstone is itself 16½ feet in length. In the late seventeenth century the cromlech was known as Coetan Arthur, or Arthur's Quoit (see Chapter 14 for other examples of sites named after King Arthur) and fairies were believed to dance here.

Pentre Ifan cromlech.

Stoney Littleton chambered long barrow, Avon

Location: 5 miles south of Bath, and in the fields of Stoney Littleton Farm (near Wellow), where the key should be collected. (ST 735572)

A low passageway penetrates almost halfway into the 100-foot mound, and this is therefore a particularly exciting burial chamber to visit, not recommended to the claustrophobic! (Take a torch, there is no light inside.) Three pairs of chambers lead off the passage, and burnt human bones have been found, with fragments of an earthen vessel. A stone with a fine fossil ammonite cast was used to decorate the entrance, its beauty obviously being appreciated by Neolithic man; but did they realise its age and the means whereby it was formed?

Clava cairns, Inverness/Highland Region

Location: 6 miles east of Inverness and 1 mile east-south-east of Culloden battlefield. (NH 757445)

Three cairns stand in a row, each encircled by standing stones. These stones are as interesting as the cairns, being particularly shapely and of an unusual textured stone. The cairns can be entered, though the central one has no passage, and all are without roofs. Only bones, pottery and flint flakes were found during excavations. Cup-marks can be seen on some of the stones. The two entrance passages align, and the alignment points to the place where the midwinter sun would have set in prehistoric times. This alignment is unlikely to be coincidental, and confirms the link between death and the sun which we noted in the introduction to this chapter.

As often happened, later peoples believed this site to be the burial place of royalty, in this case the family of King Brude.

Kilmartin cairn cemetery, Argyll/Strathclyde Region

Location: Kilmartin is 8 miles north of Lochgilphead and 27 miles south of Oban, and the cairns lie just to the west and south of the village. (Reference for most northerly site, Glebe Cairn: NR 833989)

Several cairns have been excavated and restored in this small

The interior of Nether Largie South Cairn.

area, and all of them are worth visiting. From the north they are: Glebe Cairn (cannot now be entered, but contained two stone graves, called cists); Nether Largie North Cairn (which can be entered from the top, and contains a stone burial cist, with a cover slab bearing forty-one cup-marks and carvings of axe-heads); Nether Largie Mid Cairn (two cists are visible); Nether Largie South Cairn (which is the oldest, dating from Neolithic times and having a stone-built burial chamber which can be entered; the cist visible on the edge was inserted later in the Early Bronze Age, as was a second cist no longer visible); Ri Cruin Cairn (three stone cists are exposed, one with axe-head carvings).

A short distance to the south-east of Ri Cruin Cairn is Dunchraigaig Cairn, where three cists were found; and just west of Nether Largie South Cairn is Temple Wood stone circle which must also have had a burial function as there is a stone cist exposed at its centre.

Trethevy Quoit, Cornwall

Location: 3 miles north of Liskeard, near a lane linking Darite and Tremar. (SX 259688)

Seven uprights around 10 feet high form this impressive tomb with a 12-foot capstone. The purpose of the small hole in the capstone is unknown, but the rectangular hole cut into the bottom corner of the large stone blocking the entrance was probably made to enable bodies to be placed inside.

Kilclooney More portal-tombs, County Donegal

Location: 4 miles north-north-west of Ardara, approached along a grassy lane behind Kilclooney church. (G 72 97)

Portal-tombs are very similar to dolmens/quoits/cromlechs, and are burial chambers denuded of their earth covering but

Kilclooney More portal-tombs.

still bearing a large capstone supported on uprights. At Kilclooney More two portal-tombs, one large and the other small,
are set into the remains of a long cairn. The capstone of the
larger tomb is 20 feet across, and this tomb is one of Ireland's
most impressive.

Wayland's Smithy chambered long barrow, Oxfordshire

Location: 6 miles west of Wantage, and only a short distance
west of Uffington white horse; it lies just off The Ridgeway.
(SY 281854)

Isolated in its copse of trees and beside the prehistoric Ridgeway, Wayland's Smithy seems held in a time capsule, and one
feels it necessary to keep silent when entering this ancient
grove, so as not to break the spell.

What the visitor sees today is the second phase of this tomb's
history. First of all a wooden tomb was built, paved with stone,
where bodies were placed before being sealed off and covered
by a mound. Later a larger mound was built, nearly 200 feet
long, into which at the southern end a small cross-shaped stone
chamber was inserted, where several skeletons have been found
earlier this century. Six large stones around 10 feet high were
placed across the end of the mound, these being its most
impressive feature today. Nothing of the first tomb on the site is
now visible, the whole operation dating from 3700 to 3400 BC.

The name of this tomb dates back to the tenth century and
refers to the legend of Wayland the Smith, who if a horse and a
coin were left here overnight, would shoe the horse and keep the
coin!

Capel Garmon chambered long barrow, Gwynedd

Location: 1½ miles south-east of Betws-y-Coed, and reached
along a farm track south of Capel Garmon village.
(SH 818543)

Like Belas Knap mentioned earlier, this barrow has a false
entrance. The stone burial chamber was located in the middle
of the 90-foot mound, and reached along a passage from the
side. Today it also has an entrance at the back, made when the
tomb was used as a stable in recent times. Although the
chamber is now open to the sky, a massive 14-foot capstone still

covers part of it. Because of disturbance, little has been found here – Neolithic pottery, bones and flints. As the photograph shows, the tomb is well sited, fairly high up, and with superb mountain views in clear weather.

Capel Garmon chambered long barrow.

41

3. Dwellings of early man

Evidence of domestic life in prehistoric times is scanty, but this is not surprising for, unlike the ceremonial structures, houses were not built to last for centuries. How many of our civilisation's brick boxes will still be visible in 6,000 years' time? There are, nevertheless, still enough remains to give us some idea of the different kinds of houses that were in use over a period of 4,000 years until the coming of Christianity. Before the Neolithic/New Stone Age, in the Palaeolithic and Mesolithic periods, the people are thought to have been largely nomadic and caves were used as shelters. They also used huts, of which a few traces have been found, as at Abinger Common (Surrey), where a pit, post-holes, a hearth and microlithic implements were found, dating to around 6000 BC. At the caves known to have been occupied, middens or rubbish heaps have revealed the remains of creatures long since extinct in Britain – mammoth, hyena, bear, lion, woolly rhinoceros, wolf – and traces of flint flakes, harpoons made of bone, and other items.

The settlements of Neolithic peoples have rarely survived, unlike their impressive chambered tombs and henge monuments. By far the most impressive surviving Neolithic houses are at Knap of Howar on Papa Westray island in the Orkneys (see 'Places to Visit'). Two rectangular houses lie side by side, surrounded by middens whose contents showed what food the people ate, and which helped to date the site to around 3500 BC. Modern man's rubbish tips will probably be of equal fascination to fiftieth-century archaeologists (assuming mankind survives that long).

Back in the south of England, the earliest homes to have survived date from the Bronze Age, and by contrast with the remains at Knap of Howar, are very ruinous. Because of intensive cultivation, most settlements have long since disappeared. The outlines of farmsteads, house platforms, fields, and trackways, low banks and ditches visible only to the practised eye, have been located, but in the stonier upland areas, hut circles have also survived – small circles of rocks and boulders, a number of them close together and encircled by the remains of a stone wall. On Dartmoor these settlements are called pounds, and are probably of late Bronze Age or early Iron Age date.

Moving into the Iron Age, the evidence becomes more plentiful. In Cornwall there are groups of 'courtyard houses', the best preserved example being Chysauster, each house consisting of a courtyard with small rooms leading off it. Drains, hearths, querns for grinding corn, and plenty of pottery fragments were found, enough material to enable archaeologists to build up a picture of life in such a village 2,000 years ago. Also in the Iron Age, the great hillforts were being built (see Chapter 5). Their purpose is still uncertain, but they may have had both domestic and defensive functions. Traces of huts have often been found inside them, showing that people certainly lived there. Also perhaps with a view to protecting themselves

The remains of about 150 huts can be seen inside Craig Rhiwarth hillfort near Llangynog (Powys).

against raiders, some groups of people built settlements in lakes and marshes. In Ireland, such lake dwellings (called 'crannógs') have been found to date back to the late Bronze Age, though they were mainly built in early Christian times, and some were still in use into the Norman period. They are also known in western Scotland. They consisted of artificial islands, made of stakes and brushwood, with huts built on a platform. In County Clare, a crannóg has been reconstructed, and this provides a vivid picture of an unusual type of dwelling. Such experiments can also provide much valuable information for archaeologists, as is the case at the long-term Butser Iron Age Farm Project in Hampshire (see 'Places to Visit'). Not only have authentic buildings been constructed, but people have lived there totally cut off from the twentieth century, in order to reproduce the way of life of the Iron Age farmer.

At the same time, a long way away in northern Scotland, peasant farmers were also hard at work, and as elsewhere in Britain, hillforts had been constructed during the Iron Age. However, towards the end of the Iron Age, around 100 BC, a remarkable architectural development took place, and from the earliest fortified dwellings the broch grew up. 'Grew up' literally, because a broch was a tall stone tower, 40–50 feet high. Such buildings were unique in Britain: 'not only do they represent the summit of prehistoric drystone architectural achievement, but they also seem to be the only really elaborate ancient buildings which were invented and developed entirely in Scotland' (Euan W. MacKie in his valuable book *Scotland: An Archaeological Guide*). Inside the broch was an inner wall, with between the two walls a staircase and a series of galleries one above another. Brochs were probably the equivalent of the later Norman castles, their function primarily being a refuge for the nobility in times of strife, though as with castles some may also have been permanent living quarters. A number of brochs survive in good condition, though the walls are rarely as tall as when first constructed, and the interiors are ruinous. From the broch probably developed the wheelhouse, circular stone buildings peculiar to the northern isles, examples of which can still be seen on Shetland and in the Outer Hebrides.

In Ireland, where stone forts had also been built in the Iron Age, the stone buildings often constructed inside the forts eventually developed into the characteristic 'clocháns', beehive-shaped huts with drystone walls. These were largely built during the early Christian period, and those which survive are found at religious settlements. Good examples can be seen at the early monastic settlements on the island of Inishmurray (Co. Sligo) and Skellig Michael (Co. Kerry), a rocky island and difficult of access, which is probably why the ruins are so well preserved. There are six clocháns in fine condition, with dry-stone walls 6 feet thick. Small retaining walls seen outside probably contained tiny gardens to provide a more varied diet for the monks who lived there.

The tradition of building beehive-shaped huts has been maintained in Ireland right into the present century. Only a few decades ago they were still being built, but as pigsties. The sweathouse was a very similar structure, examples of which can be found in Leitrim, Cavan, Fermanagh and Tyrone, although they are not being actively preserved, and are therefore tending to deteriorate. They are not prehistoric buildings, but date from any time since the Vikings, and were in regular use in past centuries. As their name suggests, they were the ancient equivalent of the sauna, a form of communal steam bath. Heat was built up by means of a fire for several days beforehand, then water may have been thrown on to hot stones to make steam, before small groups of people went inside the sweathouse unclothed. Afterwards they would often bathe in a nearby stream or pour water over themselves. This procedure was mainly followed as a cure for rheumatic complaints, but was probably also done to promote a feeling of well-being, as in saunas today.

One other uniquely Irish structure deserves mention here, as it is in some ways reminiscent of the Scottish broch. This is the round tower, whose tall, thin shape still dominates many religious sites in Ireland. Around sixty-five survive, though only a few are intact. (Three round towers were built outside Ireland – on the Isle of Man and in eastern Scotland – so they are not totally unique to Ireland, though virtually so.) The earliest dates from AD 940 and they are thought to have been built as belfries, watchtowers, places of refuge and, similar to church spires, as symbols of man's reaching up to Heaven. They were not really practical as long-term houses, not even as defensive shelters, because a fire lit at the base would soon burn the wooden floors and rise quickly up through the structure.

Although settlements of all ages, from the earliest cave dwellings to the Iron Age and early Christian stone structures, provide some evidence of our ancestors' lifestyle, the middens which contain the most valuable material hold only items which have not decayed, and therefore many potentially valuable items, such as clothing, are rarely found. A major discovery

Sweathouse at Annagh Upper (Co. Leitrim), built of stone and covered with sods.

during the summer of 1984 is likely to add greatly to our knowledge of Iron Age man, when the tests have been completed. This is the well preserved body of an Iron Age man, 2,500 years old and found in a peat bog near Wilmslow (Cheshire). He was lying crouched in a foetal position, and his head, trunk and a severed leg have survived. He was discovered when the men working a peat-cutting machine spotted a human foot, though not before the machine had damaged the corpse. Experts have found that 'Pete Marsh', as he has been nicknamed, was a twenty to thirty-year-old man with a ginger beard. His flesh, skin and hair have all been preserved. He had been garotted – a ligature of animal sinew was still visible round his neck. He may have been a criminal, or a sacrificial victim, or both. When the tests are finished, he will be put on display at the British Museum. It is almost certain that many other bodies lie preserved in peat bogs. In 1850 the well-preserved body of a Romano-British man was found in a peat bog on Grewelthorpe Moor (North Yorkshire). He was wearing a green cloak, a scarlet garment, yellow stockings and leather sandals. Many preserved bodies have been found elsewhere in Europe, Danish finds being described in Dr P. V. Glob's marvellous book *The Bog People*.

46

PLACES TO VISIT

King Arthur's Cave, Hereford & Worcester

Location: Above the River Wye, and reached by footpath from lanes south of the A40, near Whitchurch. (SO 545155)

Men of the Palaeolithic and Mesolithic periods (well over 6,000 years ago) lived inside this cave, later moving to the cave mouth and the ledge outside. Excavations have revealed the bones of many animals they hunted, including mammoths and other long-extinct species. Traces of fires and flint tools were also found.

Several other caves in Britain where early man is known to have lived can be visited, for example, Kent's Cavern, Torquay (Devon) where some of the items found are on show; five caves at Creswell Crags, Whitwell (Derbyshire) which were first occupied around 43,000 BC by Neanderthal Man; Gough's Cave in Cheddar Gorge (Somerset) where there is also a small museum; and Goat's Cave, Paviland (Glamorgan) where a skeleton covered with red ochre was found buried beside a mammoth skull, these and the accompanying mammoth ivory and stone tools dating back at least 18,000 years.

King Arthur's Cave was said to be the place where King Arthur hid his treasure when being chased by his enemies. Merlin the magician put a spell on the cave so that no one should ever find the treasure.

Knap of Howar prehistoric dwellings, Papa Westray, Orkney

Location: Papa Westray is to the north of the Orkney Islands, off Westray, and the Knap of Howar is on the west coast, near Holland. (NY 483519)

The two dwellings at Knap of Howar are thought to be the oldest stone houses in north-west Europe. Stone slabs divide the interiors into separate rooms, and the houses were probably roofed with turves. The largest house measures roughly 30 by 16 feet. Recesses in the walls were probably used as cupboards. Excavations revealed Iron Age material at first, but later Neolithic pottery and food refuse were found, showing that the houses were occupied as early as 3500 BC.

Other similar dwellings have been found, but none quite so old. *Skara Brae* village on Orkney Mainland has several huts clustered together, in a remarkable state of preservation. It was probably occupied first about 4,500 years ago, until around 3,000 years ago when it was suddenly engulfed by sand during a storm. Much of the furniture, being made of stone, has sur-

The interior of one of the dwellings at Knap of Howar.

vived intact – basins, mortars, cooking pots containing animal bones, stone beds, a 'dresser' with shelves – and the village was surrounded and almost hidden under its midden which has provided much information on the occupants' diet.

Also well worth visiting is *Jarlshof* settlement (Shetland), a complex site whose use extended from the Bronze Age through the Iron Age and Viking periods, a medieval farm being built in the thirteenth century and a laird's house in the sixteenth century. As at Skara Brae the site was covered by sand, its presence unknown until a storm in 1897 exposed part of it. Courtyard houses, a broch, wheelhouses and Norse houses have been excavated.

Grimspound settlement, Devon

Location: 7½ miles north-west of Ashburton, not far east of a minor road crossing the moor north–south between Chagford and Widecombe. (SX 700809)

Dartmoor today does not look the most inviting of locations for a cattle farm, but in the late Bronze Age conditions may have been better. Grimspound survives as evidence for such settlements, and a ruined wall encloses a large area in which can be seen the remains of about twenty-four huts and some cattle-pens. The name 'Grimspound' was given to this place when it was already ruinous and its occupants forgotten – 'Grim' means the Devil, or Woden, or some evil spirit.

Chysauster prehistoric village, Cornwall

Location: 3 miles north of Penzance, along a lane to the west of the B3311. (SW 472350)

Several houses can be entered, each with a central courtyard off which are small rooms where domestic rubbish and pottery were found during excavations. Hearths and drains were also found, and workrooms and cattle sheds. Each house had a terraced garden with a low stone wall, and terraced fields were constructed on a nearby hill-slope. These people were obviously farmers, but they also supplemented this by an early form of industry, as is shown by a track leading from the settlement to a stream where tin working was carried out. Chysauster was occupied from 100 BC to the third century AD, during the time the Romans were in Britain, but their influence hardly extended into the lives of these peasant farmers and tin-workers.

Not far away, near Sancreed, is *Carn Euny* village, first settled in 200 BC. The inhabitants followed the same pursuits as at Chysauster, including tin-working. This village also has huts which have been excavated, and an additional feature of great interest, a 65-foot-long underground passage called a fogou or souterrain (see Chapter 9).

Din Lligwy village, Anglesey, Gwynedd

Location: Near the east coast, 6 miles south-east of Amlwch and
reached by footpath from a lane north of Llanallgo.
(SH 497861)

Several ruined huts, circular and rectangular in shape and enclosed by a stone wall, survive from this settlement which was occupied in the late fourth century AD. The round huts were dwellings, the rectangular ones were iron-smelting workshops.

The site is tucked away, hidden by trees, and very atmospheric if you are alone there. Very close at hand are two other places of interest, a ruined medieval chapel and a prehistoric tomb, the gigantic capstone weighing about 28 tons.

A well-preserved circular dwelling hut at Din Lligwy.

Mousa broch, Shetland

Location: On tiny Mousa Island, off the south-east coast of
Shetland Mainland and reached by boat from Sandwick.
(HU 457237)

Although needing determination to reach it, this broch is well
worth the effort, as it is the best preserved, still standing over 40
feet high. It is a fine example of architecture and workmanship.
The first $12\frac{1}{2}$ feet is of solid drystone construction, and 50 feet in
diameter. Above this it is constructed of two drystone walls
joined together by six stone galleries, the gap between the walls
being wide enough to comfortably walk along. Access to the
galleries and wall top is by a spiral stair which is also between
the walls. But the galleries were probably not the living quarters, these were at the bottom of the hollow inner core which
originally had a wooden floor above ground level, and a roof
above that. A wheelhouse was later constructed within this
inner area. Later still, when the broch was already an antiquity,
it provided refuge for Norse fugitives, an eloping couple who in

1153 stocked the tower with stores and barricaded themselves inside against their pursuers.

Other well preserved brochs in the Orkney and Shetland islands include:

Broch of Gurness (Orkney Mainland: HY 383268) which had outer defences in the form of three rock-cut ditches; Iron Age debris was found. Later a courtyard house was built and, later still, a Viking long-house.

Midhowe broch (Rousay Island, Orkney: HY 371308), similar to the Gurness broch and also with external defences; it was later adapted for domestic use and some of the stone was used to build huts close by.

Broch of Burland (Shetland Mainland: HU 446360) On a cliff promontory and worth seeing for its situation and as a broch that has not been excavated; the outer defences are massive, and the broch wall is in part still 10 feet high.

Clickhimin (Shetland Mainland, at Lerwick: HU 404132) At this complex and important site are the remains of a courtyard house, a massive outer wall, a 'block-house' fort and a broch, with a later wheelhouse inside.

Carn Liath broch, Sutherland/Highland Region

Location: 2 miles north-east of Golspie, and beside the A9, between the road and the sea. (NC 871013)

The entrance to Carn Liath broch.

Many of the well-preserved brochs are relatively inaccessible, being on islands off the north and west coasts of Scotland, but there are also a few on the mainland, and Carn Liath broch is probably the easiest to reach, lying close to a main road. This fact of course tends to lessen the atmosphere of the place; nevertheless it is still well worth visiting. The walls still stand 12 feet high in places, and the entrance passage and lintelled doorway are impressive. Remains of the internal stair can still be seen, and there are two deep stone-lined pits in the floor, one of them 8 feet deep and thought to have been a well. Ruins of buildings outside the broch suggest that a settlement grew up once it was no longer necessary to maintain a defended fort.

Other notable brochs on the Scottish mainland include *Dun Dornadilla*, Loch Hope, Sutherland (NC 457451), still 20 feet high at the entrance; *Dun Telve*, Inverness (NG 829172) and, close by, *Dun Troddan*, with surviving walls up to 32 feet high. *Dun Carloway broch* on the Isle of Lewis, Outer Hebrides/Western Isles (NB 190413) should also be mentioned, for its location as well as its considerable remains. Details of other brochs worth visiting can be found in Euan W. MacKie's *Scotland: An Archaeological Guide*.

Anyone interested in the down-to-earth practicalities of life in earlier times should pay a visit to those places where prehistoric and later settlements have been reconstructed. These include:

Butser Ancient Farm, Hampshire

Location: On Butser Hill in one of Hampshire's Country Parks, 3 miles south-west of Petersfield. (SU 717203)

At Butser an Iron Age farm dating to around 300 BC has been built, with round-houses made of wattle and daub and with thatched roofs, and another hut of turf. Authentic crops such as woad, flax, beans and cereals are being grown, with animals used for ploughing and pulling carts, and the breeds of cattle and sheep are as close as possible to those which Iron Age farmers would have kept. The Project Director, Peter J. Reynolds, has written interesting books giving full details of the experiment and what has been learnt from it.

The Craggaunowen Project, County Clare

Location: 9 miles east-south-east of Ennis and 3 miles east-south-east of Quin; signposted. (Q 46 73)

Kilmacduagh round tower.

Because of their location surrounded by water, the remains of genuine crannógs are difficult of access, and the surviving remains not visually impressive. A circular crannóg complete with nuts in the style supposed to have been used at such settlements has been recently built in County Clare, and at the same location there is also a 'new' stone-walled fort of the kind found in Ireland.

Saxon village, West Stow, Suffolk

Location: The nearest village is Flempton, $4\frac{1}{2}$ miles north-west of Bury St Edmonds. (TL 808710)

During excavations, traces of eighty timber buildings were found at West Stow, together with domestic items like pottery, combs, weaving tools and jewellery. The way of life of the inhabitants could be pieced together from the surviving evidence, and the site excavator decided as an experiment to reconstruct examples of the buildings which had stood there around 1,300 and more years ago. Split tree trunks were used for the walls, the gaps being filled with clay; the roofs were thatched. The result is houses which were pleasanter to live in than we might at first imagine – go and see for yourself!

54

Round tower at Kilmacduagh, County Galway

Location: 3 miles west-south-west of Gort. (M 40 00)

It's not easy to miss this tower, which stands almost 100 feet high and has a Pisa-like lean. It is one of the best preserved round towers in the country and is set among several ruined buildings, churches and a cathedral, the remains of a monastery founded in the seventh century. Closer examination of the ruins will reveal some fine carvings – a cross-slab in the north wall of St Mary's church (across the road), and other carvings on the chancel arch and east windows of O'Heyne's church (the farthest from the tower).

Other fine examples of round towers can be seen at Glendalough (Co. Wicklow), Donaghmore (Co. Meath), Monasterboice (Co. Louth), Kilree (Co. Kilkenny) and at many other places (for more details see Anthony Weir's *Early Ireland*).

4. Enigmatic standing stones

The reasons for the erection of single standing stones are as enigmatic as are the reasons for the construction of stone circles. There are hundreds of standing stones throughout Britain and Ireland, often single stones, sometimes in groups of three or four. Some are very tall – the tallest in Britain is the impressive Rudston monolith (Humberside) nearly 26 feet high, while Ireland has a 20-foot stone needle at Punchestown (County Kildare) – others are very small and thus unnoticeable in the bracken or heather of the upland regions where they are most often found. Although little is known about them, one thing is certain: that they were erected for a purpose. One of the more prosaic suggestions is that they were cattle rubbing posts. Some erected in recent centuries may well be so, but many are too tall and heavy, or too short, to be suitable for this, and most standing stones are thought to have been erected in the late Neolithic and Bronze Ages. Possible uses in those times were as route markers, burial markers, boundary markers, and to mark mineral outcrops.

Often the standing stones were not placed in isolation, but close to stone circles or as part of a group of several similar stones. If some stone circles were used as astronomical observatories, then the associated standing stones may have been the markers for sight lines towards distant hills where the sun, moon or planets became visible over the horizon. Some stones have had holes bored through them, which may also have been used for making precise astronomical observations. In more recent centuries, by clasping their hands through the hole two people would solemnly seal an agreement such as the exchange of marriage vows. Such a practice indicates the continuing veneration of the stones throughout the centuries. Some stones have been seen as phallic symbols, being used by barren women as sources of fertilising energy, through the practice of simple rituals (see our book *Earth Rites* for more information). Whether this symbolism was intended or even noticed by the

people who originally erected the stones is impossible to ascertain; though as we have noted elsewhere, the alternating diamond and pillar stones sometimes found, as in the Kennet Avenue (Wiltshire), are thought to have symbolised the female and male principles.

The shape of standing stones is a fascinating study. A similarity has sometimes been noticed between the outline made by a prominent hill on the skyline and the shape of a nearby standing stone, and more examples of such similarities may await discovery. We have observed this similarity ourselves, and John Sharkey also noticed it when studying the standing stones at Callanish (illustrated in Chapter 1) – 'the actual curves of some of them mirror the shape of the distant hilltops'. This may have been done simply for aesthetic reasons, it may have had some significance in rituals connected with astronomical observations, or it may have had some esoteric significance we are not aware of. If, as some people suspect, the whole system of erecting stone circles and standing stones was intended in some way to channel or utilise the natural energies inherent in our environment, then the careful shaping of the standing stones

A holed stone known as the Bole Stone at Crouse (Wigtown/ Dumfries & Galloway Region).

57

A standing stone near Kinnerton (Powys), whose shape echoes that of the Whimble in Radnor Forest, seen on the skyline.

may have been done with a definite purpose. It certainly does suggest some link between points in the landscape, which is also the basis of the ley theory (for more details, see Chapter 19). Apart from this echoing of the surrounding hills, many if not all standing stones have been carefully shaped for some purpose. Was this art or science? Or was it a supreme blending of both? – a skill which later generations have increasingly ignored, to their peril.

Where several standing stones are grouped together, they have often been placed in a line. If many stones are used, the line can become an avenue formed by a double line of stones, the most impressive example of this now known being at Avebury (Wiltshire). Here it seems very likely that this avenue (and a similar second avenue now destroyed) was used as a processional way (see Kennet Avenue in 'Places to Visit'). This cannot have been the case with the less visually impressive but more enigmatic stone rows, the best examples of which survive on Dartmoor in Devon. The stones are often less than 3 feet tall,

58

and the rows, sometimes double or even triple, often lead to or from a cairn or round barrow. The other end may be 'blocked' by a single standing stone. In some cases, these rows are up to 1,000 feet long. Their purpose remains unknown.

Somewhat different from the standing stones and stone rows are the stones known as 'inauguration stones', once used in the installation of chiefs and kings, though possibly some standing stones may have been used for a similar purpose in prehistoric times. Perhaps the best known inauguration stone in Britain is the Stone of Scone, which became headline news in the early 1950s when Scottish Nationalists removed it from its present resting place beneath the Coronation Chair in Westminster Abbey, London, and whisked it off to Scotland. Since 1297 all British monarchs (with the exception of Mary I) have been crowned while seated above it, and before them Scottish monarchs were crowned on it when it was located at Scone (Perth/Tayside Region). Fortunately it was retrieved and returned to Westminster Abbey so that the ancient rite can continue without hindrance.

A number of other similar blocks of stone used as inauguration stones were known of in recent centuries, and a few may well have survived though such stones could easily be discarded as being of no significance if not protected by those who know their true value and history. (Other examples are described and illustrated in our earlier book *The Secret Country*.) Some inauguration stones carry carved footprints, upon which the king or chief placed his feet to make his vows during his inauguration ceremony. Sadly, since little interest has been shown in these stones as compared with the visually imposing prehistoric sites, many of them have been destroyed or lost, a fact we should all regret. One lost example was a footmarked slab on Islay (Strathclyde Region) where the Lords of the Isles are said to have been inaugurated; this was destroyed in the seventeenth century. Two examples of stones still preserved are at Dunadd and Clickhimin (see 'Places to Visit'). Why were these stones so important in the inauguration ceremony? Were they simply part of an age-old ritual, or did they produce a significant change in the new leader? It is probable that, by standing on a spot sacred to the clan or tribe, where his predecessors had stood, the new king or chief was ritually becoming part of an unbroken line of authority and leading the clan forward into the future. He would also become revitalised by making contact with the earth at this long-hallowed place, thus enabling him to carry out his function with wisdom and energy.

59

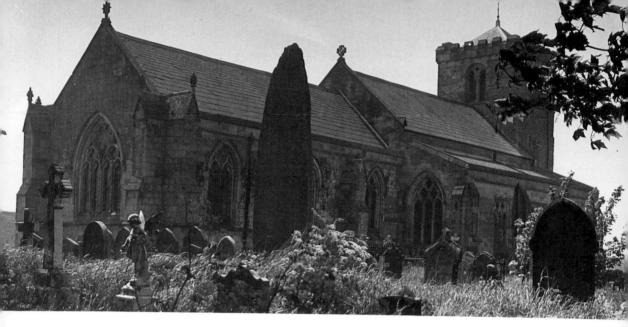

Rudston monolith.

PLACES TO VISIT

Rudston monolith, Humberside

Location: In Rudston churchyard, 5 miles west of Bridlington.
  (TA 098677)

Apart from being Britain's tallest standing stone at 25 feet 9 inches (and it may have originally been nearer 28 feet, as the top seems to have been damaged), the location of this monolith ('single stone') in a churchyard serves to tell us that this site was considered sacred long before the Christians established a church there. If this stone was erected early in the Bronze Age, it stood here for at least 2,500 years before the site was first used for Christian worship. As we shall see in Chapter 11, Christians often adopted pagan sacred sites, either in recognition of the sanctity of the site, or in a desire to destroy any lingering paganism. But if it was the latter, why did they not demolish the stone? A legend explains the close proximity of stone and church by saying that the stone was hurled by the Devil with the intention of demolishing the church; whereas obviously the stone was there first and the church builders for some reason decided not to demolish it. The relationship between the early Church and the supporters of the pre-Christian religions, the so-called pagans, is shrouded in mystery: there seems to have been an unexpected mutual tolerance.

60

The Devil's Arrows, North Yorkshire

Location: Between Boroughbridge and the A1, 6 miles south-
east of Ripon. (SE 391665)

Three standing stones, which are almost but not quite in a line,
in legend represent more of the Devil's projectiles, this time
thrown with the intention of destroying the early Christian
settlement at Aldborough, but as usual he missed his target,
and the Arrows still stand in open fields, the tallest being 23 feet
high. All three bear deep grooves from the top, and were
presumably artificially shaped to look like this, just as the
shapes of the stones themselves were determined by their erec-
tors, though some people believe that the grooves have been
caused by natural weathering. It seems that the stones were
brought from Knaresborough 6 miles away, itself a major
undertaking. A St Barnabas Fair used to be held in a field near
the stones on the summer solstice, probably a continuation of
ceremonies held here in prehistoric times.

The Longstone and stone rows on Shovel Down, Dartmoor, Devon

Location: 3 miles south-west of Chagford. (SX 660857)

The Longstone, a 10-foot standing stone, stands close to several
stone rows and one double row actually ends at the Longstone.
It is not known whether the stone was originally erected
upright, or at its present angle.

   Close to the Longstone can be seen three double stone rows,
two of them beginning or ending at small cairns. The stones are
unimpressive visually, but these lines of stones on the barren
moorland will leave the visitor with a feeling of puzzlement.

The Longstone.

Nine Stones, Derbyshire

Location: On Harthill Moor, 3 miles south of Bakewell, reached from a minor road between Alport and Elton. (SK 226626)

The Nine Stones were also known as the Grey Ladies, and were said to dance at midnight. Whether there were once nine stones here is unknown, though there were six when an excavation was carried out in 1847. The stones may once have been part of a burial chamber, or a stone circle, though they seem rather close for that. One of the stones is grooved like the Devil's Arrows.

Castlenalaght alignment, County Cork

Location: 3½ miles north-by-west of Bandon. (W 49 61)

Four stones, the largest over 10 feet tall, stand in a line in a prominent location with fine views. Their purpose is unknown, but there is a burial structure about 400 yards away to the north, with a large boulder on three supporting stones, and perhaps the two sites have some connection.

Castlenalaght alignment.

Carreg standing stone.

Carreg standing stone, Gwynedd

Location: 1 mile east of Harlech, beside a lane from Llanfair to
Talsarnau. (SH 599309)

This is one of the rare instances where the purpose of a standing
stone can be deduced with a strong likelihood of accuracy.
Carreg is one of thirteen similar stones in this area, beginning in
Llanbedr village to the south, and then roughly following the
line of the lane beside which Carreg lies, ending at Moel
Goedog, where there is a fort, hut circles, cultivation terraces
and ring cairns. The standing stones are thought to have
marked a safe route across this mountainous countryside.

Kennet Avenue, Wiltshire

Location: 6 miles west of Marlborough; the avenue follows the
line of the lane running south from Avebury towards West
Kennet and the A4. (SU 103699)

The Kennet Avenue was originally 1½ miles long and connected

Kennet Avenue.

the Sanctuary with Avebury henge. The stones of the northern section have been re-erected and about thirty pairs of stones can now be seen. They are around 10 feet tall and form an avenue 50 feet wide. The most intriguing feature of the avenue is that the stones alternate in shape, a tall pillar being followed by a broad lozenge, these shapes being thought to symbolise the male and female principles. A second avenue originally ran westwards from Avebury, but it was destroyed in the eighteenth century. These avenues were possibly processional ways used in the Avebury rituals.

The Hill o' Many Stanes, Caithness/Highland Region

Location: 4 miles north-east of Lybster, beside a lane north-west off the A9. (ND 295384)

The name describes the site, but without giving any hint as to the meaning of all these small stones, over 200 of them erected in twenty-two parallel lines. Professor Alexander Thom has interpreted the hill as an astronomical observatory, which makes this visually unimpressive site an important place, if his interpretation is correct. A fallen standing stone on a ridge to the west could also have been part of the observatory, being used to locate the most southerly point of the moonrise behind distant Durn Hill.

64

The King Stone or Coronation Stone, Kingston-upon-Thames, Greater London

Location: Near the Guildhall in the town centre.

It is claimed that seven Saxon kings were crowned at this stone during the tenth century, but this is disputed in some quarters. The stone was originally located in the Saxon Chapel of St Mary, but since 1730 it has had several outdoor locations, moving in 1936 to its present site. Whatever its true history, it has now assumed a role as the relic from which the town took its name.

Inauguration stone at Dunadd fort, Argyll/Strathclyde Region

Location: 4 miles north of Lochgilphead. (NR 837936)

The first fort built on this rocky hill dates back to the Iron Age, but the most important settlement took place in the Dark Ages when Dunadd is thought to have been the capital of the Scottish kingdom of Dalriada, founded around AD 500 by Irish settlers. High on the hill, on a rocky ridge, can be seen several rock carvings – an Ogham inscription, unfortunately now unintelligible (see Chapter 6 for an explanation of 'Ogham'), a boar in Pictish style ('Pictish symbol stones' are also described in Chapter 6), a footprint and a basin. The last two are thought to have been used in inauguration ceremonies, the kings of Dalriada standing in the footprint and water which had collected in the basin being used to anoint them. Another inauguration site in Scotland was located at Clickhimin (Shetland), where a pair of footprints cut into a stone slab can be seen.

On the summit of Dunadd the carvings are exposed to the weather, which is why the boar has been protected. To its left can be seen the footprint, and to its right the basin.

5. Hillforts:
strongholds of the chiefs

Stone forts or brochs have already featured in Chapter 3, as a special form of defended settlement found only in the north of Scotland and on the Scottish islands. Elsewhere in Britain and Ireland, banks and ditches were most often used to form the defences of the many thousands of hillforts which must have been built over the centuries, several thousand of them still surviving in good condition. Most hillforts date from the Iron Age, that is after around 600 BC, though the earliest hillforts were being built in the late Bronze Age. Even further back, in the New Stone Age around 3500 BC, causewayed camps were constructed which may have been the early precursors of the hillforts. Banks and ditches broken by causeways were constructed on hilltops, the best known example being Windmill Hill near Avebury (Wiltshire). From evidence found there, in the form of more than 1,300 Neolithic pots, objects of flint and stone, and animal bones, some having been deliberately buried in the ditches, it would seem that the camp was used for some kind of ritual gathering rather than as a defensive settlement.

It was to be another 2,500 years before hilltop earthworks were used as defensive sites, though in the meantime small settlements and individual farmsteads must surely have been constructing some form of protection for themselves, against raids by wild animals on their livestock and the occasional bandit. Being small in scale, and often in lowland areas which have since been intensively cultivated, the remains of such humble fortifications as a bank, ditch and wooden stockade fence are scanty, only the earthworks having survived if at all. Such remains are now being discovered through tell-tale crop-marks, photographed from above, and it is becoming evident that in early ages the river valleys and other lowland sites were heavily settled and farmed, to a degree not before imagined, since all the visible remains so far found have been in upland areas. In Ireland, 30,000 or 40,000 of the so-called ring-forts were erected in the 2,000 years up to around AD 1200. They

The fort on Ham Hill (Stoke-sub-Hamdon, Somerset) is one of the largest in England, but it has been much damaged by quarrying. Here we see one of the outer ditches and ramparts.

were also called raths, and consisted of a farmstead protected by a simple water-filled trench.

With the passage of time, the people must have felt a more urgent need to band together in settlements which could be defended in periods of danger. The earthworks of the average-sized hillfort could not have been thrown up overnight. Planning was needed, and many thousands of man-hours of labour. Maiden Castle (Dorset) covers around 45 acres and the inner circumference is $1\frac{1}{2}$ miles, though admittedly that is a particularly large fort and developed in several phases. The big forts like Maiden Castle were skilfully designed and constructed, and were successful in keeping out invaders, Maiden Castle only falling about AD 44 to the might of a Roman army under Vespasian. Traces of huts inside many hillforts show that they were used as settlements, though whether continuously or intermittently is not known.

There are nevertheless some puzzling features if the hillforts were to be successful militarily. Some of them do not appear to have had wells, which would surely be necessary for the survival of the occupants in siege conditions. Also, the larger forts like Maiden Castle, with its circumference of $1\frac{1}{2}$ miles, would have required a great many men for its defence, as a lookout would constantly have to be kept for raiders. Some of the forts,

67

the so-called contour forts, follow the contours of the land and thus enhance the natural lines of a hilltop so effectively that it has been suggested that what appear to be defences may in fact have had entirely another purpose – landscape architecture for aesthetic reasons, or as a system for controlling and channelling the flow of natural earth energies. (This is a subject we will return to in Chapter 19.) Although it would appear that hillforts were built with defence in mind, it must not be forgotten that we in the twentieth century view these sites in the light of our own experience, which has in the last few centuries involved almost constant warfare. People may not have been so belligerent in the time before the Romans arrived in Britain. In fact, as we have already noticed, there is no evidence for large-scale defences at all in the pre-Iron Age years, except for causewayed camps, and these were probably not built as defensive structures anyway. Perhaps we should think of these sites, whose common name 'hillfort' tends to prejudge the issue, more as tribal gathering places, where the people would meet regularly to trade, to follow religious rituals, to socialise. When danger threatened, which may have been rarely until the advent of the Romans, they would congregate at their local gathering-place, and unite to defend themselves against their common enemy. Some hillforts may also have been used as grain-stores.

Local gatherings at hillforts continued into recent times in some places. A fair was held at Yarnbury hillfort (Wiltshire) until early this century; and at Burrough Hill hillfort (Leicestershire) an annual event was still popular in the sixteenth century as noted by antiquary John Leland: 'To these Borow Hilles every year on Monday after White Sonday come people of the country thereabout, and shoot, run, wrestle, dance, and use like other feats of exercise.' There are many other similar examples on record.

In addition to the most frequent hilltop 'forts' in which the earthworks or defences follow the contours of the land, there were several other kinds of fort to suit other types of terrain. In low-lying areas, plateau forts would be constructed, employing one or more sets of banks and ditches. Promontory forts were projections of land with steep slopes only needing the addition of banks and ditches across the strip of land linking the promontory to the surrounding land. By the sea, where steep cliffs were the main defence, promontory forts are known as cliff-castles. These are most numerous in Ireland, where the dramatic coastline of the south and west is ideally suited for fortification. Around 200 such forts can be identified, and the defences were

The ruined stone wall which once protected the north side of Craig Rhiwarth hillfort above Llangynog (Powys); to the south is a steep cliff.

massive dry-stone walls. Because of the ease with which it could be obtained, stone was very widely used in Irish forts, and stone-wall defences were the Irish equivalent of the banks and ditches used elsewhere. Some of the walls still contain staircases and chambers. Four Irish forts included *chevaux-de-frise* among their defences – a 'paving' of stones laid sharp end up so that the attackers' horses could not cross to the ramparts. A few examples of this have also been found in Wales and Scotland. This system of defence may have been more widely used, employing pointed sticks of which no trace now remains.

Timber was widely used in the construction of defensive ramparts in those areas where it was plentiful, and one result of this is the so-called 'vitrified forts'. These are the subject of considerable controversy, some people believing the vitrification was accidental, others that it was deliberate. The latter theory is that ramparts were constructed of stone with a timber filling, the wood then being ignited and the resulting intense heat causing the stone to melt, thus forming a solid rampart of fused stone. Other archaeologists feel that the ramparts would have been vulnerable to fire, perhaps because of a drier climate, and the burnings were initiated either by attackers or accidentally by the defenders. However the fires began, there is no doubt that a very intense heat would be needed to cause the stone to melt. Vitrification has occurred too widely for anyone to deny that it could happen, but how it came about is still not really understood.

Around 2,500 hillforts survive in good condition on the British mainland, and visiting them is a healthy pursuit strongly recommended to the more energetic of our readers. We can only give a small sampling in 'Places to Visit', but about 150 of the most interesting forts on the British mainland are described in detail in A. H. A. Hogg's *Hill-Forts of Britain* which is also a good general introduction to the subject, and the best of the Irish forts feature in Anthony Weir's *Early Ireland: A Field Guide*.

PLACES TO VISIT

Maiden Castle, Dorset

Location: Just south of Dorchester, reached via Maiden Castle Way off the A354. (SY 670885)

Maiden Castle has few rivals, and would be near the top of

anyone's list of 'The Seven Wonders of Ancient Britain'. Photographs hardly do it justice – you really need to walk the 1½ miles round the top of the ramparts to properly appreciate the magnificent achievement of the men who conceived and constructed it. Having said that, we should explain that Maiden Castle was not the result of one man's vision, but developed gradually over many years. Around 3000 BC, a Neolithic causewayed camp was built on the eastern side of the natural hill, and later a large burial mound was erected on the same area. Around 2,500 years after the hill was abandoned, about 350 BC, a small hillfort was constructed, again on the east, which soon fell into disrepair and then suddenly the fort was repaired and enlarged. At this time a foundation sacrifice was laid in a pit, a young man whose skeleton was found during excavations this century.

Within 200 years the fort again needed restoration, and this time the ramparts we see today began to take shape. Double ramparts were dug to the north, and treble to the south, and the inner rampart was dug very deep, 50 feet from the top of the bank to the bottom of the ditch. The entrances were made even more elaborate than they were already. The eastern entrance has been excavated, and platforms for slingers and sentry boxes

Even after nearly 2,000 years of erosion, the banks and ditches of Maiden Castle remain impressive.

71

were discovered. Beside one was a pit containing 22,260 sling-stones from nearby Chesil Beach. The fort may now have seemed impregnable, and we do not know how many on-slaughts it may have withstood from around 100 BC until it was finally overrun in about AD 44, by the Romans. During the later construction phases, the interior of the fort was occupied, much evidence being found in those areas that were excavated. After the Roman attack, the inhabitants were allowed to stay on at the fort, but it was finally abandoned around twenty years later and a new settlement grew up at what is now Dorchester.

This much is known about Maiden Castle's history as a result of a large excavation conducted there by Sir Mortimer Wheeler during 1934–38, many of the finds being on display at Dorchester Museum. These include part of a backbone with a Roman arrowhead embedded in it. A war cemetery was found dating from the time of the Roman attack, with thirty-eight bodies, many of the skulls showing clear sword cuts. To mark the World Archaeological Congress in Britain in 1986, a major new excavation is to be carried out under the direction of Dr Geoffrey Wainwright, who has said: 'We hope this new excavation will tell us much more about who lived inside the fort prior to the siege and why, and its earlier history in Neolithic times. We also want to reinstate the ramparts of the fort, one of its most striking features, but which have been eroded in recent years.'

Knockfarrel vitrified fort, Ross & Cromarty/ Highland Region

Location: 2½ miles west of Dingwall, but much farther in driving distance, being approached along narrow lanes from the south. (NH 505585)

A lump of vitrified rock on Knockfarrel fort.

The hilltop crowned by this fort is littered with lumps of vitrified rock, so it is a good place to examine easily the results of the vitrification process, and to try to imagine the scene on this now peaceful hilltop at the time when the fort's defences burnt so fiercely that the rock melted. It hardly seems feasible, but a tremendous temperature must have been generated, because there is the vitrified rock to prove it!

Old Oswestry hillfort, Shropshire

Location: Just north of Oswestry town, and reached along a lane off the A483. (SJ 295310)

Around the western entrance there are seven ramparts, but these were not constructed all at once. There were no fortifications at all around the small settlement of wooden huts which formed the first phase of development, possibly around 300 BC. Later the many ramparts were built in several phases up to about AD 100. Although Old Oswestry was traditionally known as Caer Ogyrfan, Gogyrfan's Fort, Gogyrfan being the father of Guinevere who was the wife of King Arthur, the date of the pottery found there shows that it was impossible for this to have been their home, and so, in the words of A. H. A. Hogg as he demolishes a fanciful legend, we 'must now regretfully abandon the romantic vision of King Arthur riding through the ruins of the great west entrance to visit his future in-laws'.

Worlebury Camp, Avon

Location: At Weston-super-Mare, with the town to the south and the sea to the north; the fort can be approached from the south or the east. (ST 317626)

Easily reached from the town and well worth visiting for a walk through the woods which now cover it, Worlebury Camp is also an important hillfort, though the trees tend to hide its details. Most easily seen are the remains of stone walls originally 35 feet thick and still more than 10 feet high, but looking at first glance like piles of discarded rubble. They were once defensive walls of elaborate construction, but they did not finally keep the attackers out – skeletons have been found bearing signs of violence, possibly the result of a Roman attack. Also still visible are the many overgrown holes in the ground, ninety-three of them having been discovered. They were storage pits and were found to contain many items like pottery, spindle whorls, sling

73

stones, iron spearheads and charred grain. The local museum houses many of the finds.

Rubh' an Dunain galleried dun, Isle of Skye/Highland Region

Location: Towards the south of Skye, on the coast, opposite Soay Island, and reached on foot. (NG 396160)

This must surely be one of the most remote sites in this book and makes a vivid contrast to those forts which stand close to a large settlement, such as Worlebury Camp. There are not even any roads within several miles of Rubh' an Dunain, but the determination needed to reach it will certainly be rewarded. The fort is a galleried dun or semibroch perched on a clifftop promontory, and takes the form of a curved stone wall 12 feet thick and still standing 8 feet high, cutting off the promontory. Small fortlets like this one were being built in Scotland at the end of the Iron Age, and they preceded the development of the larger and more elaborate brochs, hence the name 'semibroch'.

Rubh' an Dunain galleried dun.

Tre'r Ceiri hillfort, Gwynedd

Location: On the Lleyn Peninsula, just west of Llanaelhaearn and best reached from the west at SH 360437, the end of a minor road north of Llithfaen.

A mountain top 1,500 feet above sea-level seems an unlikely place to build a village, but perhaps the winds blew less briskly and the weather was warmer when 'the town of the giants' was first occupied. A stone wall still standing 13 feet high encircles the settlement, and inside are the remains of many huts. These vary in design, with circular huts, subdivided circles, D-shapes and rectangles, and some have been dated to between AD 150 and 400, but others may be much earlier than that. The first structure to be built on the hill was a cairn dating from the Bronze Age, around 1500 BC. Enclosures on the hill-slope were probably small paddocks for the sheep and cattle kept by the inhabitants. They do not seem to have grown many crops, as no querns for grinding corn have been found, but the terrain close to the fort is hardly suited to arable farming, being very stony. As with most hilltop forts, the views on a clear day from Tre'r Ceiri are stupendous, across the sea and along the peninsula.

Barbury Castle, Wiltshire

Location: 4 miles south of Swindon, in Barbury Castle Country Park. (SY 149763)

In a county rich in ancient sites, including a number of fine hillforts, Barbury Castle is one of the most impressive. It covers 12 acres and has two outer ditches. Iron Age chariot fittings, jewellery and agricultural implements have been found, and aerial photography has revealed hut circles and storage pits. Traditionally Barbury Castle is the site of the Battle of Beranbyrig, AD 556.

Mote of Mark hillfort, Kirkcudbright/Dumfries & Galloway Region

Location: At Rockcliffe, 4 miles south of Dalbeattie. (NX 845540)

The details of this fort on a rocky hill are difficult to see because of the natural growth and tumbled boulders, but there are

Mote of Mark hillfort.

traces of a massive stone wall now vitrified. The fort was first built in the late Bronze Age or early Iron Age, and finds show that it was in use until the second century AD, iron smelting and metal working being carried on there. It was later reoccupied in the eighth and ninth centuries. As the photograph shows, the fort is in a commanding position overlooking Rough Firth.

Herefordshire Beacon hillfort, Hereford & Worcester

Location: On the southern section of the Malvern Hills, reached from the car park opposite the British Camp Hotel, on the A449. (SO 760400)

This is a fine example of the type of hillfort that makes one wonder if some of them were after all constructed for aesthetic reasons rather than defensive. The bank and ditch follow and emphasise the contours of the hill, the result being an enclosed area of 32 acres seemingly difficult to defend successfully

76

because of the length of the rampart. The first fort here was only 8 acres in area, on the highest point of the hill, where much later in the twelfth century AD a medieval castle mound was built.

Whatever its true origins, Herefordshire Beacon hillfort is a fine place for a walk, especially on a windy day! It hardly seems possible that people could really have lived in this exposed spot, unless the weather was much gentler or the people extremely tough.

A small section of Herefordshire Beacon hillfort, with the ridge of the Malvern Hills beyond.

Staigue fort, County Kerry

Location: 7 miles east-south-east of Waterville and 2 miles north of the main road to Sneem. (V 61 63)

This is a fine example of a stone fort, with the wall still standing 17 feet high. A lintelled doorway also survives, and in the wall can be seen stairways leading to terraces, and passages leading to corbelled cells.

6. *Ancient rock art: hidden messages?*

Today the most familiar forms of expression are the written and spoken word, both of which are vital to our civilisation. Music and art are more subtle forms of expression, but still of vital importance to the well-being of mankind. Indeed, we could all well do without a large proportion of the words which deluge us daily, but our civilisation would be impoverished if we lacked the best of music and art. In prehistoric times there was, so far as is known, no written word, and the spoken word may have been confined to intimate person-to-person communication. Music there may have been; art there definitely was. The prehistoric rock carvings which have survived in some of the Neolithic passage tombs, in Ireland especially, are rich and beautiful, skilfully executed and still able to evoke admiration today. The best examples are found at Newgrange, Knowth, Fourknocks and Loughcrew, two of these sites being featured in 'Places to Visit'.

Whether the great variety of designs used were simply chosen for their aesthetic qualities or also possessed religious and spiritual significance is difficult to assess, though Martin Brennan, who has meticulously studied the most elaborate of the carvings in the Boyne Valley, sees them as Stone Age sundials (to much simplify his detailed work), used by the scientists of the day to study the solstices, equinoxes and movements of the moon. Such a suggestion is no longer as outrageous as it would once have been: recent research into the sky lore of the original peoples in all parts of the American continent has shown beyond question that they were advanced watchers of the sky, and had constructed all manner of devices to help them observe and plot the celestial movements. In many details these devices bear very close resemblance to the carvings of the New Stone Age in Ireland. For example, spirals are often seen in the Irish tomb art, and at Fajada Butte in Chaco Canyon, New Mexico, two spirals were found carved on a rock. At noon at the summer solstice a researcher saw a sliver of sunlight shine between slabs

78

of stone standing against the rockface and move vertically through one of the spirals. She was able to show that this was not a coincidence, for at the equinoxes a dagger of light crossed the other, smaller, spiral. It is very likely that some at least of the prehistoric carvings in Ireland and elsewhere in Europe had a similar astronomical function.

Decorated lintel-stone inside Fourknocks passage-tomb (Co. Meath). Martin Brennan sees this as a 'Neolithic scientific instrument for charting the sun's movements'.

Apart from the tomb art, there are many other prehistoric rock carvings which are difficult to interpret but some of which may have had an astronomical function. Cup and ring marks predominate, and these could be sun symbols. They are carved on slabs of rock in the open air, and possibly date from the Bronze Age. One interpretation is that they are magical symbols carved in an attempt to bring back the sun at a time of cloudier weather and a generally deteriorating climate. Other symbols are also seen – cup marks without rings, concentric rings, crosses, lines crisscrossed and meandering, etc. These petroglyphs (i.e. rock carvings) are found throughout Ireland and in Britain, especially in the Isle of Man, Northumberland, the Yorkshires, Galloway and Argyll.

The explanations for the carvings are almost as numerous as the carvings themselves – Ronald W. B. Morris lists 104 explanations in one of his books, and a number of them could be valid: alignment markers, marks made by early copper and gold prospectors, magical symbols (representations of parts of the

79

mother goddess's body, fertility symbols, etc.), water diviners' symbols, mixing vessels (for casting bronze, mixing colours, etc.), measures, cups for Druidical blood sacrifices, early clocks, written messages, maps of the countryside or the stars, doodles, boundary markers, route markers, gaming tables, memorials to the dead, weathering of natural rock strata, oath or victory marks, knife-sharpening marks, and so it goes on. The carvings are certainly intriguing, and a lifetime of study could be devoted to them, but at present we lean to the belief that some of them, particularly the cup and ring marks, had an astronomical function, possibly as magical symbols intended to bring back the often-absent sun. If the weather was deteriorating, as seems to have happened in the late Bronze Age beginning around 1000 BC and continuing over several hundred years, this would have had dramatic consequences both for agriculture and astronomical observations which relied on clear skies, and the people's temporal and spiritual practices and beliefs would have been thrown into chaos.

The people of later ages continued to carve strange symbols on to rocks and stones, and in two important cases these have been shown to be genuine scripts, and have been deciphered. One of them is called Ogham, a very strange script thought to have originated in Ireland and based on the Latin alphabet. Straight or slanted lines were used in different combinations to represent letters, their positioning along a straight-edge, usually the edge of a stone, also being very important. For example, the vowels are formed of one, two, three, four or five short lines across the edge; Q is four lines to the left of the edge, N is four lines to the right, and so on – see the photograph of Lewannick Ogham stone in 'Places to Visit' for an illustration of how Ogham looks in use. The name Ogham (or Ogam) comes from Oigmiú, who was the smith-god and the god of writing, and it was often used for memorial inscriptions on stones in the late Iron Age. It was in use from AD 300 to the end of the seventh century, and over 300 stones with Ogham inscriptions are now known, in Wales, Cornwall and Scotland as well as Ireland.

Equally strange are runes. The runic script was brought over to Britain from Scandinavia in Saxon times, and was actively used between the fifth and eleventh centuries AD. It was used on monuments including crosses, gravestones, coins, and on any object that bore decorative carving. As might be expected with a script of Scandinavian origin, monuments and objects with runes are to be found largely in the north and east of England, with also a few examples in south-west Scotland. The symbols used are difficult to describe, but an idea of their appearance can be gained by studying the accompanying illustration.

The Norse god Woden was, according to myth, the discoverer of runes and so they were a magical alphabet not used for everyday communications. They could be engraved on to personal objects such as rings and swords, and carved on to stones and caskets. The rune master was the wise man who was skilled in the use of these hieroglyphs and only he would know the correct characters to use to give protection and power to both the object and its owner. With the coming of Christianity the use of runes was adopted by the monks and runic and Latin scripts were used together on monuments and coins. The Ruthwell cross (Dumfries & Galloway) is a good example of this blending of the pagan and Christian practices, part of the Anglo-Saxon poem 'Dream of the Rood' being carved in runes on one side of the cross.

Runes are carved down the edges of the east and west faces of the Ruthwell Cross.

Some of the most beautiful and fascinating forms of ancient rock art are known as 'Pictish symbol stones', which are unique to Scotland. The Picts were a group of tribes living in north-east Scotland *c.* AD 300–850. The earliest of their 'symbol stones' were standing stones incised with the emblems which make them uniquely Pictish – such things as mirrors, combs, snakes or serpents, animals, birds, fishes and geometrical shapes, all rendered in a firm yet delicate outline of great beauty and precision. The meaning of these symbols is uncertain, but mirrors and combs suggest women, and some of the stones are thought to have been tombstones. After AD 700 the stones became more elaborate. Instead of being unworked blocks of stone incised with a few designs, they took the shapes of Christian cross-slabs and the designs were carved in relief, the usual Pictish designs now being accompanied by Christian symbols and interlace ornament (see the Aberlemno churchyard stone in 'Places to Visit'). These later stones illustrate the spread of Roman Christianity into previously Celtic areas. The best examples are works of art to rival the Celtic crosses we shall see in the next chapter.

Even though the Pictish symbol stones are so much nearer to our own time than the earliest rock art we have described, only 1,200 years ago as against 5,500 years ago, they are equally mystifying. We can recognise some of the symbols, but why they should be carved on stones in this way is not known. Many of the symbols are still unidentifiable. One animal, described as an elephant-like creature, may in fact be a representation of water monsters which were seen in those days, and may still be seen, in the Scottish lakes. The best known of these creatures today is the Loch Ness Monster, which some people believe still inhabits the large lake near Inverness (see Chapter 20, where there is a photograph of the monster). The Pictish animal has a 'proboscis' projecting from its head which could be the appendage looking like an elephant's trunk which some witnesses of water monsters have reported seeing, and other features of the Pictish creature bear a close resemblance to features of Nessie and her cousins as reported by modern witnesses. Since a whole range of animals and birds is accurately depicted on the symbol stones – wolf, bull, cow, stag, horse, eagle, goose – perhaps these were the creatures most familiar to the Picts in their everyday world, and 'monsters' were also familiar to them, being more often seen in the lakes than they are today, and accepted as part of the natural world just like eagles and stags. Unlike today, when the monster's very existence is hotly debated!

PLACES TO VISIT

Newgrange passage-tomb, County Meath

Location: 3 miles south-east of Slane; signposted. (O 00 72)

We have already included Newgrange in the 'Places to Visit' in Chapter 2 as a burial site, but in this entry we concentrate on its decorated stones, which are among the finest examples of pre-historic rock art in Europe. Over a dozen of the stones lining the passage are decorated, also some roof-slabs and corbels. The triple spiral illustrated here is on one of the uprights in the chamber. As a design it shows dynamic balance, but we shall never be sure exactly what metaphysical concepts it may have

Newgrange triple spiral.

Newgrange kerbstone.

encompassed. Many of the kerbstones which surround the exterior of the mound are also decorated, both on their outer and hidden faces, the most impressive being the stone shown here, which is on the far side of the mound from the entrance stone (itself illustrated in Chapter 2).

Loughcrew passage-tombs, County Meath

Location: 10 miles west-by-north of Kells, on two hilltops in the Loughcrew Hills. Cairn T is locked, the key being obtained from a house south of the car park. (N 57 77)

Of the 50–100 tombs once visible at Loughcrew, many have been destroyed but a number still survive, and in them can be found a wealth of rock art. Cairn T is particularly well preserved and worth visiting.

Derrynablaha petroglyphs, County Kerry

Location: 1 mile east of Lough Brin, in the Ballaghbeama Gap. (V 77 78)

On over twenty rocks on a rocky hillside can be seen some fine examples of cup and ring marks. Please consult Anthony Weir's *Early Ireland: A Field Guide* for precise instructions on how to locate the right rocks!

Derrynablaha petroglyphs.

Roughting Linn petroglyphs, Northumberland

Location: 3 miles north of Doddington, beside a lane off the
B6525, near Roughting Linn farm. (NT 984367)

A sloping rock surface is decorated with over sixty carvings of
various designs, and this is probably the best display of prehistoric rock art in England. There are good individual examples
elsewhere, but nowhere so many all together in one place.

Lewannick Ogham stone, Cornwall

Location: Lewannick is 4 miles south-west of Launceston, and
the stone stands inside the church. (SX 276807)

The inscription on this memorial stone is in Latin as well as
Ogham, and translates as 'Here lies Ulcagnus'. There is a
second Ogham stone in the churchyard at Lewannick, though
because of long exposure to the weather the Ogham characters
are less clear. The inscription reads 'To the memory of Incen-
vus'.

Lewannick Ogham stone.

Trallong Ogham stone, Powys

Location: Trallong is 5 miles west of Brecon, and the stone is
inside the church. (SN 966296)

This Ogham stone was found in use as a window lintel when the
church was restored in 1861. The Latin and Ogham inscriptions read 'Here lies Cunocenni son of Cunoceni', and the stone
has been dated to the fifth or early sixth century AD. A Latin
ring-cross was added later, on the part of the stone that was
buried in the ground when it was serving its original purpose as
a gravestone or memorial.

Aberlemno Pictish symbol stone, Angus/Tayside Region

Location: The stone shown here is in Aberlemno churchyard
(there are others by the roadside); Aberlemno is 5 miles
north-east of Forfar. (NO 523555)

There are three symbol stones at Aberlemno, of which the best
example, and also one of the finest anywhere in Scotland,
stands close to the church. It is an intricate cross-slab made

85

from sandstone. One side carries the cross and intertwined beasts; on the other side is a battle scene, with the soldiers' armour and weapons still clearly detailed.

Aberlemno Pictish symbol stone: cross face.

Aberlemno Pictish symbol stone: battle face.

Turoe Stone, County Galway

Location: 4 miles north-north-east of Loughrea, in a field at Bullaun. (M 63 22)

This strangely shaped and carved stone is a superb example of Celtic art, and its shape is suggestively phallic, indicating that it may have represented the male principle in ceremonies and rituals which are now lost to us. Its similarity to the Castle-strange stone in County Roscommon (M 82 60), which may be a female stone, is striking, and we surmise that stones such as

86

these were used in the ever-important fertility rites. This description is necessarily vague, for there is nothing definitely known about these stones, and so they are tantalising in the extreme. Whether the beautifully convoluted whorls were simply surface decoration or whether they held an intrinsic meaning related to the ceremonies performed at the stones is very much a matter for conjecture.

In his book *The Ancient Science of Geomancy*, Nigel Pennick notes the similarity of the Turoe Stone to the Delphic Omphalos Stone, which marks the centre of the Greek world, 'omphalos' meaning 'navel'. The carvings may symbolise the harnessing of the site's energy.

Turoe Stone.

Sueno's Stone, Moray/Grampian Region

Location: On the outskirts of Forres, beside the B9011. (NJ 047595)

Few people have ever heard of Sueno's Stone, although it is, as Euan W. MacKie describes it, 'one of the most remarkable Dark Age sculptured stones in Britain, if not in Europe'. It is thought to commemorate a battle victory 1,000 years ago, for the back shows four scenes of soldiers on foot and on horseback, battles, bodies, a procession, and a building like a broch. Every surface of this 23-foot pillar is carved and ornamented, and on the front is a wheel-cross with decorative interlace. Sueno for whom it is named may have been a Norseman defeated near this spot by the Picts. Alternatively a recent book, *The Symbol Stones of Scotland* by Anthony Jackson, argues that Sueno's Stone commemorates a defeat of the Picts by Kenneth Macalpine, *c.* AD 842.

Sueno's Stone.

7. The cross, symbol of eternal life

A typical Cornish wayside cross, Three Holes Cross near Wadebridge.

Although the cross is now assumed to be a wholly Christian symbol, it has been used by many cultures in different ages. It was used on Bronze Age burial artefacts some 4,000 years ago; the Egyptian ankh was a cross; to the Maoris the cross was the moon goddess; to the Maya the tau cross was the Tree of Life; to the Buddhists the cross was the axis of the Wheel of the Law, and there are many other similar instances around the world. The cross is a universal symbol with many possible shades of meaning, and it fitted very well as a symbol of Christianity, since Christ's Crucifixion on a cross was the central point of the religion, and the cross thus came to symbolise salvation through Christ's sacrifice. When Christianity came to Britain, a simple cross was often carved on to stone monuments, including standing stones, the intention presumably being to exorcise the pagan associations of the stone, and to convert it to Christian use. Crosses were also added to other early carved stones, such as Ogham stones (see Chapter 6; Trallong Ogham stone, for instance, has an added cross).

From these simple beginnings, Christian crosses gradually became more elaborately decorated, especially in areas of Celtic influence. At first the crosses were carved on stone slabs, but not all the early crosses were intended to stand upright. Some were grave-slabs, designed to lie flat above the grave of the person commemorated. Some early Christian gravestones did stand upright to mark the grave, and this custom which we still employ today may have had its origins in prehistoric times, since some Bronze Age standing stones have been found to stand adjacent to burial cists containing cremations and so were probably intended as burial markers or gravestones. These are particularly common in Cornwall, with others in Wales and Ireland.

Later, the stones were sculpted to take the shape of a cross. The decoration became very elaborate, and included biblical scenes. The acme of cross carving was reached in Ireland

89

possibly during the ninth and tenth centuries (the dating is uncertain), high crosses being found at many monastic settlements, and today many fine examples can still be seen. A few of these high crosses were funerary monuments, but most of them were commemorative monuments. Elaborately carved Celtic crosses are also found in Wales, while elsewhere in Britain many crosses survive whose designs show a variety of influences, including Celtic and Saxon. Cornwall is particularly rich in early Celtic-influenced crosses, especially the westerly half of the county where a great many round-headed granite crosses can be seen. Many are near churches, but others in isolated locations may have been intended as route-markers for pilgrims.

In northern England, there are hidden away in churches many fragments of Anglo-Saxon sculpture dating from the period when the Vikings were influential in Britain, and close study of the scenes depicted on these cross fragments reveals scenes from pagan Norse mythology. Experts have been able to trace the interactions between these pagan themes and early Christian beliefs. There is also Viking sculpture on the Isle of Man, which before the ninth century had a Celtic Christian population. As a result of Scandinavian immigration, the Viking influence became predominant and the Celtic was submerged.

In the Middle Ages, crosses with steps at their base were erected in churchyards, at cross-roads, in market-places, on village-greens. Preachers would preach from them; villagers would lay out their wares for sale on them (the more elaborate butter crosses had a roof for protection against the weather); they were also used as boundary markers and meeting places, and as points from which to measure the distances between towns.

Churches of course were decorated with crosses of many kinds, inside and out, including the gable cross on the roof. Less conspicuous were the small crosses incised on the exterior wall; some were consecration crosses, others were meant to keep evil spirits away. Protection against evil spirits may also have been the function of the gable cross, and of the grotesque beasts whose heads are often seen decorating church walls.

This elaborate cross is a friars' preaching cross from the fourteenth century, and the only surviving example of its type in England. It is in Hereford, beside the ruined Blackfriars, the home of the Friars Preachers.

The cross has continued in active use to the present day, as a universally accepted symbol of Christianity. Churchyards have many cross-shaped gravestones, and war memorials are often copies of Celtic designs, but the modern efforts lack the supreme artistry of the superb crosses of 1,000 years ago.

Cross-slab at Meifod, Powys

Location: Meifod is 5 miles north-west of Welshpool; the
cross-slab is inside the church. (SJ 155132)

The date of this beautifully carved tombstone is uncertain: one
expert suggested ninth or tenth century, another felt it might be
the tombstone of one of the Princes of Powys and date from
around 1160. The design shows a number of influences. Below
Christ crucified and a Maltese cross in a circle is a Latin cross
encircled with knotwork, with examples of Celtic plaits and
Viking knots interspersed.

Meifod cross-slab.

St Brynach's Cross, Nevern.

St Brynach's Cross, Nevern, Dyfed

Location: In the churchyard at Nevern, which is 7 miles south-west of Cardigan. (SN 083401)

This fine Celtic cross stands 13 feet high, close to the church. It dates from around AD 1000. There are also some earlier carved stones at Nevern: a fifth–sixth century stone with Latin and Ogham inscriptions beside the porch, another Ogham stone inside the church, and a tenth-century cross with Viking design, again inside the church. A consecration cross can also be seen on the outside of the building, on the north side.

Maen Achwyfan, Clwyd

Location: In a field beside a lane 1 mile north-west of Whitford and 4 miles north-west of Holywell. (SJ 129787)

This is a Northumbrian style of cross, with Scandinavian elements in its design, but being so far west it also shows clear Celtic influence. Its date is tenth–eleventh century.

Maen Achwyfan.

Briamail's Cross, Llandefaelog Fach, Powys

Location: In the church at Llandefaelog Fach, 2 miles north-
west of Brecon. (SO 034324)

This 8-foot cross-slab bears a Latin cross, below which is a
figure possibly holding a club and a dagger. The inscription
reads '+ Briamail Flou', and the slab has been dated to the late
tenth century.

Saxon cross at Bewcastle, Cumbria

Location: Bewcastle is an isolated settlement in wild country
9 miles north-north-east of Brampton, but the cross is easily
found in the churchyard. (NY 565746)

In Saxon times, the kingdom of Northumbria (which encompassed northern England from the Borders south to Yorkshire)
was a great artistic centre. This cross is one of the best surviving
examples of Northumbrian art, though sadly it now lacks its
head. The 14½-foot shaft is covered with interlace, inscriptions

Briamail's cross.

Saxon cross qt Bewcastle.

and figures, including St John the Baptist with the Agnus Dei, Christ in Majesty, and St John the Evangelist. There are runic inscriptions between the panels, but they are too worn to be translated. Some people believe that the cross may commemorate King Aldfrith who reigned in Northumbria from AD 685 to *c.* 704. He was a scholar and patron of the arts, and may have died at Bewcastle.

Saxon cross at Eyam, Derbyshire

Location: Eyam is 6 miles north of Bakewell, and the cross is in the churchyard. (SK 218765)

Several fine crosses can be seen in the Saxon kingdom of Mercia, this being the best preserved. Eyam is close to the frontier between Mercia and Northumbria, and so not unexpectedly the carving on the cross shows a mixture of styles from the two kingdoms. It is clear that at some time the shaft was broken, and the head placed on what remained. The spiral design on the shaft is reminiscent of the triple spiral carving in

Saxon cross at Eyam.

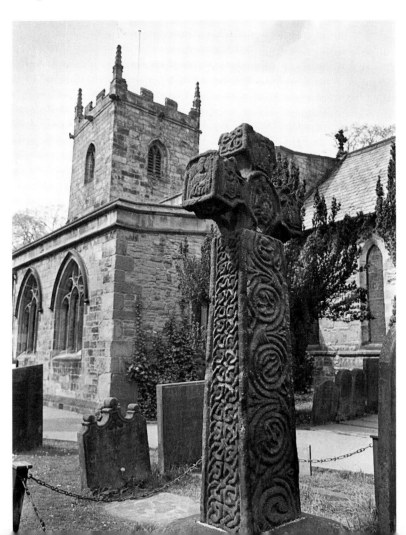

Newgrange passage-tomb (see Chapter 6), and is also similar to the Cardinham cross shaft design (illustrated elsewhere in 'Places to Visit').

Saxon cross at Gosforth, Cumbria

Location: Gosforth is 12 miles south of Whitehaven, and the cross is in the churchyard. (NY 072036)

This fine and well-preserved Saxon cross depicts the conflict still raging between the old and new religions around the tenth century. Elements from Norse mythology are shown, including dragons, wolves and interlaced beasts, together with the Christian symbols of the cross-head and a carving of the Crucifixion, the whole being taken to represent the victory of Christ over the pagan gods.

Celtic crosses at Llantwit Major, South Glamorgan

Location: Llantwit Major is 9 miles west of Barry, almost on the south coast; and the crosses are in the church. (SS 966687)

St Illtyd was head of a monastery and school of divinity established at Llantwit Major (formerly known as Llanilltyd Fawr) in the fifth century, where many early saints and other famous

Celtic crosses at Llantwit Major.

men were probably educated, including St David, Gildas the historian, and Taliesin, the Welsh bard. From the ninth to the eleventh centuries, Welsh kings were buried at Llantwit Major. As a reminder of the town's early Christian associations, a collection of fine Celtic crosses dating from the ninth to the eleventh centuries can be found in the church. The 6-foot cross shown in the photograph, decorated with fret and interlace patterns, carries an inscription at the base which translated reads: 'In the name of God the Father, and of the Son and of the Holy Ghost. This cross Houelt prepared for the soul of Res his father'. Houelt was probably Hywel ap Rhys, a ruler in this area in the late ninth century. The other crosses also carry inscriptions commemorating kings like Samson, Juthahel, Artmail and Ebisar.

Not too far away from Llantwit Major is another collection of crosses, in the old school close to the abbey at Margam. The earliest cross dates from the sixth century, but those of the ninth and tenth centuries are the most elaborate and richly decorated, especially Conbelin's Cross.

Cross at Cardinham, Cornwall

Location: Cardinham is 3 miles north-east of Bodmin, and the cross stands in the churchyard by the porch. (SX 123687)

Cardinham cross.

Though now worn, the designs of interlace, spirals and ring-chain are still clear, and together with the attractive shape make this a fine cross. The ring-chain is the same as used on the Isle of Man by a sculptor named Gaut (Gaut's Cross can be seen at Kirk Michael on the island). The Cardinham cross probably dates from the tenth century.

Ruthwell Cross, Dumfries/Dumfries & Galloway Region

Location: Ruthwell is 6 miles west of Annan, and the cross is inside the church, to the north of the village. (NY 101682)

This cross dating from the late seventh century has been described as one of the major monuments of Dark Age Europe. In the seventeenth century it was broken into two pieces and buried beneath the church on the order of the General Assembly of the Church of Scotland. Later it was dug up and restored, more pieces having been broken off, and now the side arms are replacements. A pit was dug in the church floor to accommodate it, and it is now the dominant feature inside the small building.

Among the scenes depicted on the cross are St John with the eagle, St John the Baptist with the Agnus Dei, the Flight into Egypt, Christ performing miracles, the Crucifixion, and Christ in Glory. As described in Chapter 6, text of the poem 'Dream of the Rood' is carved in runes down the edges of the side panels. Other inscriptions are in various scripts including Anglo-Saxon capitals and insular minuscules.

Crosses at Monasterboice, County Louth

Location: Monasterboice is 5 miles north-west of Drogheda, and the crosses are in the graveyard, where there is also a round tower. (O 04 82)

There are two fine crosses to be seen here, known as Muiredach's Cross and the West or Tall Cross (20 feet high). Both are covered with carvings of biblical scenes and ornamented designs. They may date from around AD 840, and Muiredach was the name of two local abbots and a local king. Ley enthusiasts (see Chapter 19) will be intrigued to know that Monasterboice aligns with Tara (ceremonial site) and Knowth (passage grave), both in County Meath.

The central carving on the west face of the Tall Cross shows the Crucifixion, surrounded by other biblical events such as Judas's Kiss and Christ's Baptism. This cross and others of a similar kind are topped by miniature chapels or shrines of cruck-construction, the study of which provides evidence for early church design.

99

8. Dykes and tumps, moots and mottes

Fenny Castle Hill near Wookey (Somerset), a Norman motte and bailey.

Apart from the earthworks we have already described, burial mounds (Chapter 2) and hillforts (Chapter 5), the observant traveller through the countryside will have noticed other mounds of earth obviously ancient but not fitting into the categories of either burial mound or hillfort, and seemingly inexplicable. In fact some are ancient, others are more recent; some are inexplicable, others are easily explained. We must start with the biggest: the biggest mound and the biggest mystery – Silbury Hill (Wiltshire). This is the largest manmade hill in Europe, and completely unlike any other prehistoric

earthwork. Archaeologists have always thought that it must be the burial place of some very important person, but despite three excavations, no trace of any burial has been found. For other, more esoteric, suggestions which have been made, see the description in 'Places to Visit'.

Work began on Silbury Hill in the Neolithic period, and possibly of the same age is the enigmatic type of earthwork known as a cursus. No examples of these are given in 'Places to Visit' as they are visually unimpressive. The Dorset cursus extends for 6 miles and consists of two parallel banks with outer ditches, the ends closed by banks and ditches. There are a number of barrows close by, and archaeologists think that the cursus had an astronomical significance or was connected with a prehistoric cult of the dead, but there are no real clues to its meaning. Equally puzzling is the cursus near Stonehenge, which consists of one bank and ditch, about 1½ miles long and 110 yards wide. The nearness to Stonehenge suggests that its use was associated with that monument; the eighteenth-century antiquary William Stukeley thought it might have been a chariot course. A cursus was also found at Thornborough (North Yorkshire), over which a henge had later been constructed, and doubtless there were others which may have been destroyed by centuries of cultivation.

The bank forming a cursus was probably never very high, and they are unlikely to have been constructed as a boundary or defence. Other banks and ditches survive which may have played these roles, and they are known as dykes. Most of these were built much more recently, during the Saxon period. Offa's Dyke, possibly the best known of these earthworks, was built in the late eighth century and extends roughly along the length of the Welsh border. It was probably built to define the westerly frontier of Mercia, rather than being intended as an impregnable defence to keep out all the Welsh: it would be impossible to keep such a long earthwork permanently manned. Shorter earthworks have been built along other sections of the Mercian frontier. In East Anglia, dykes were built around Cambridge, possibly to try to hold back eastward incursions from Mercia. Farther south, Wansdyke (Wiltshire) may have been built to divide Wessex from the Mercians. All earthworks of this kind cannot be assumed to be of Saxon date, for earlier dykes do survive. Grim's Ditch (Berkshire) dates from the Iron Age. It was quite a long dyke across the Berkshire Downs and Chiltern Hills, probably delineating a boundary. Both Wansdyke and Grim's Ditch are named after Woden the Norse god who among

The mysterious earthwork beside Llyn Gwyn (Powys).

his many attributes was the god of warriors.

Late in the eleventh century the Normans overran England, and in order to maintain control they built many castles. The earliest of these survive in the form of earth mounds called mottes. On the flat top a wooden structure was built, and of course these have not survived. The motte was usually a cone-shaped mound, sometimes a reinforced natural knoll. A ditch surrounded it, and adjoining it was an enclosure surrounded by banks and called the bailey. The motte was the refuge and watch tower for the soldiers; the horses and food were kept in the bailey. Some variations on this basic design can sometimes be confused with prehistoric earthworks. On the Welsh border, a motte is often called a tump; in Wales, tomen.

In later centuries, abandoned mottes were good places to hold local festivities. Flat-topped mounds were also convenient sites for moots or meetings, held mainly to deal with local legal and administrative affairs. Sometimes the meetings were held at crossroads, boundary meeting points, hillforts, prominent trees or stones or hills. Sometimes existing flat-topped mounds were used, sometimes the tops of barrows were flattened for this purpose, and sometimes special mounds were constructed. Look out for names like Moot-lowe or Mutlow, which indicate the former site of a moot.

Another type of earthwork which at first sight looks ancient and mysterious but in fact has a reasonable explanation is the

102

so-called pillow-mound. These are low, oblong mounds around 2–3 feet tall, 50–90 feet long and 20–40 feet across. They are found in groups, and for some while their age and purpose were unknown, but they are now thought to have been artificial rabbit warrens, dating from medieval times onwards. Rabbits were once very important for their meat and fur, though nowadays it is hard to believe that they needed to be encouraged to breed by the provision of artificial warrens! Good examples can be seen at Llanfihangel nant Melan (Powys) where there are over thirty on a slope, and Thetford Warren (Norfolk).

Not all earthworks have yet been identified, however. There are many strange-shaped earthworks in the countryside whose date and purpose remain unknown. One example is shown here, a semicircular bank beside Llyn Gwyn near Nantmel (Powys).

PLACES TO VISIT

Silbury Hill, Wiltshire

Location: Beside the A4, 5 miles west of Marlborough. (SU 100685)

Silbury Hill is close to Avebury and the West Kennet long barrow, and visible from both. Whether this has any significance is not known, though it seems likely that the three sites were somehow linked. Speculation as to the meaning of Silbury Hill is widespread, because the archaeologists have failed to prove their theory that it was built as a tomb for a high-ranking prehistoric chieftain. It certainly was not built on an idle whim. It has been estimated that the mound, which is 130 feet high and 100 feet across at the top, took 18 million man-hours to construct. The first phase dates from 2500 BC when a 16-foot mound was built. It was soon enlarged; then the plan was changed and a much larger mound was constructed in steps. Finally the steps were filled in to give a smooth slope.

The first excavation in 1776 consisted of a shaft dug down from the summit. In 1849 a tunnel was dug into the centre from the base of the mound, but nothing was found. Professor Richard Atkinson redug this tunnel in his 1968–70 excavations, through which much was learnt about the construction of the mound. But no one found any trace of a burial. It may still await discovery, perhaps hidden off-centre. Or Silbury may have had

According to one legend, Silbury Hill was made by the Devil who was building Wansdyke and wiped his spade, thus forming Silbury Hill. This photograph of the hill was taken from West Kennet long barrow.

an astronomical function. If so, its construction serves to demonstrate the importance of astronomical observations to the people of that time. Other suggestions include a gigantic sundial, with a large pole erected on top of the hill – though why go to all the trouble of building such a huge mound for this purpose? Michael Dames in his book *The Silbury Treasure* saw Silbury as a representation of the winter goddess. In folklore King Sil is buried there, on horseback and clad in gold. There is only one fact of which we can be certain: that Silbury Hill is the largest manmade prehistoric mound in Europe.

Twt Hill, Rhuddlan, Clwyd

Location: Rhuddlan is 2 miles south of Rhyl, and Twt Hill is beside the River Clwyd, and behind the castle, reached along a lane to the east of the castle. (SJ 026776)

Twt (pronounced 'toot') Hill is now overshadowed by the considerable ruins of the thirteenth-century castle at Rhuddlan. It is a motte, the site of an early Norman castle erected in 1073 by Robert of Rhuddlan, 'the terror of North Wales'. There is a fine view from the top of the motte, over the River Clwyd and its meadows.

Bass of Inverurie, Aberdeen/Grampian Region

Location: In the cemetery at Inverurie, and close to the river. (NJ 781206)

This is a very well preserved Norman motte, 50 feet high, now incongruously located in a cemetery. It has a smaller mound, the Little Bass, by its side.

Bass of Inverurie.

Tump Terret, Trellech, Gwent

Location: Trellech is 4 miles south of Monmouth and Tump Terret can be found in a farmyard in the centre of the village, not far from the church. (SO 499054)

From its shape it is highly probable that this mound was a Norman motte. It has remained in a good state of repair,

105

perhaps because of the traditional belief that a calamity would befall anyone who excavated it. In folklore it was said to be the burial place of all the warriors who died in the battle commemorated by Harold's Stones not far away. These three standing stones, which probably date from the Bronze Age, gave the village its name, as Trellech means 'village of stones'.

Tump Terret, Trellech.

Wansdyke, Wiltshire

Location: The dyke stretches 45 miles from Bristol to Marlborough, but is not now visible throughout its length. The most complete. section is in the east, SU 030670 to SU 195665.

The name of this earthwork means 'Woden's Dyke', Woden being an important Anglo-Saxon god from whose name is derived the word 'Wednesday'. It is generally thought that the dyke was built by the Saxons to mark the boundary of Wessex, or as a defence against the Mercians who had a tendency to southerly encroachment. However, there is no real evidence that the Saxons built it; it could have had its origins in an earlier boundary dispute. The easterly section near Marlborough passes through some fine countryside and its course can be followed for 10 to 15 miles.

Wansdyke on Tan Hill (Wiltshire).

Offa's Dyke, eastern Wales

Location: Along the Welsh border from Chepstow in the south to Prestatyn in the north. The best stretches are on the mid-Wales/England border, north of Knighton, around Montgomery, and south of Chirk.

King Offa of Mercia was responsible for this feat of construction around the late eighth century, to delineate Mercia's western boundary. The dyke was massive when first constructed, much more impressive than it is today, much of it having been eroded or ploughed down during the succeeding centuries, though along some stretches the bank still stands high. It is likely that it was also intended to deter the savage Welsh from raiding the farms in western Mercia, though it would surely have been an impossible task to permanently man the dyke along its length. Perhaps lookouts kept a check on the activities of the Welsh, and reinforcements were called in when large-scale raids seemed imminent.

One of the best defined stretches of Offa's Dyke, seen following the curve of Llanfair Hill above Llanfair Waterdine on the Powys/Shropshire border.

The history and purpose of the dyke are still far from clear, and excavations continue annually at different sections along its length, and also at short dykes which exist on the Welsh side of Offa's Dyke, for example the Upper and Lower Short Ditches in the Kerry Hills. The more energetic among our readers can walk the length of Offa's Dyke along the Long Distance Footpath, which is now a popular walk. However, the continual tramp of human feet along the top of the bank, together with the activities of livestock and wildlife, are now resulting in severe erosion of the dyke in some places.

9. *Underground Britain*

Humanity has always had a fascination for caves and underground passages, even to the extent of creating artificial underground places to satisfy an undefined inner need. The earliest men lived in caves, as we have already described in Chapter 3. The caves in Britain where they lived were very simple when compared with the complex cave systems in southern France where the famous cave paintings dating back many thousands of years have been discovered. Even when more civilised housing was available, some people still preferred to live in caves, even into recent centuries. Saints and hermits have often chosen caves as shelters, for example St Ninian's Cave, near Whithorn (Wigtown/Dumfries & Galloway Region), where early incised crosses can be seen on the cave walls.

The entrance to a souterrain on Hirta, St Kilda (Western Isles), a remote group of islands to the west of Lewis.

The earliest artificial caves seem to have been the passage tombs constructed in Neolithic times. The eerie experience of entering one of these can be relived today, especially at a tomb with a particularly long passage such as Stoney Littleton long barrow (Avon), or Camster round cairn (Caithness/Highland Region) whose passage is 20 feet long and less than 3 feet high at the centre of the cairn. Although one purpose for which these structures were made was as tombs, as we have already seen in Chapter 2, they are likely to have played a multiple role, of which the resting place of the deceased was only one, and perhaps not even the most important.

The symbolism incorporated in the design of the passage grave was of great significance, as it was an entry into both the underworld and the Earth Mother's womb. By placing the dead within, they were returned to the womb of the Earth from whence they had originally come, to await a future rebirth. This concept of death and rebirth may have been depicted by some of the carvings found inside the tombs. Possibly the flowing circles of the Newgrange triple spiral expressed the idea of the soul following a spiral of evolution from one centre of incarnation out and back into the next.

Natural and artificial caves may also have been used for initiation ceremonies, such as are still performed in some societies in remote areas of the world. In North America the rites of initiation were performed in underground chambers called kivas which were built and used by the North American Indians until recent times. In prehistoric Britain, sheltered by the protecting walls of earth and rock and surrounded by reminders of the venerated tribal elders long dead, Neolithic initiates may have received instruction inside the passage graves from the tribal shamans, undisturbed by the distractions of the outer world.

Underground chambers and passages were also dug in search of certain substances needed to support a way of life. Inside Cissbury Ring hillfort (West Sussex) more than 200 depressions mark the site of Neolithic flint mines which were 40 feet deep. These date from nearly 6,000 years ago, and had long been abandoned by the time the hillfort was constructed in the Iron Age. At Grimes Graves in Norfolk, today's visitors can actually climb down into one of the flint mines (see 'Places to Visit'). Other early mining activity which took place underground included the search for gold, and the Roman gold mines at Dolaucothi (Dyfed) can also still be seen.

During the late Iron Age and the early centuries AD (and also

111

much later, in some parts) intriguing underground passages called variously souterrains, fogous (in Cornwall), earth-houses and weems (in Scotland) were built. Cornwall is the only English county where they are found, and in Scotland the main concentration is in Angus and Orkney. None are known in Wales, but many were built in Ireland, even as late as the thirteenth century at Ballybarrack in County Louth. Often found in conjunction with settlements, their purpose is thought to have been domestic – as cattle sheds, or foodstores, perhaps for dairy produce which would keep better in cold conditions. When danger threatened, they could also be used as refuges. In parts of Ireland where cattle-raids were frequent, souterrains were probably built primarily as refuges.

There is no evidence to suggest that souterrains ever had any religious significance, but it is certainly possible that some may have been built for this reason. In Ireland they have sometimes been dug into the mounds of passage-graves, but there may be no significance in this location: it may simply be that the mounds were easier to dig into than the rocky ground. In Scotland, most of the surviving Angus souterrains are now roofless (e.g. Tealing, Ardestie and Carlungie) which enables interior details to be clearly seen, but spoils the atmosphere. By contrast the two restored souterrains on Orkney Mainland are positively claustrophobic, that at Grainbank being entered along a passage 26 feet long, but less than 3 feet wide and 3 feet high. Inside Rennibister earth-house were found human bones and skulls, indicating that it was used as a tomb when it was no longer needed for domestic purposes. Shells mixed with black earth were found in the passage, suggesting its use as a rubbish dump.

In early Christian times, small underground chambers called crypts were sometimes built beneath churches. These were used for the burial of notables such as kings, as chapels, or as places to house precious relics. The crypt at Hexham (Northumberland) dates back to c. 680, and is the major surviving part of the early church of St Wilfrid. Other notable Saxon crypts worth seeing are at Repton (see 'Places to Visit'), Wing (Buckinghamshire) and Ripon (North Yorkshire). There are fine crypts in three Norman churches – Lastingham (North Yorkshire), St Peter-in-the-East, Oxford, and Berkswell (West Midlands) – and in five cathedrals, Canterbury, Worcester, Gloucester, Rochester and Winchester. If, as seems possible, the church building is a focus for earth energies, the crypt would logically be the area wherein these energies were most

The crypt beneath Canterbury Cathedral (Kent), unaltered since its construction around 1100.

concentrated. It is sometimes possible to sense the pulsing energy currents inside a church, and our own most dramatic experience of this was in the Norman crypt at Lastingham which we must have entered at just the right moment to catch a highpoint in the energy cycle, which caused a kind of explosion inside our heads. On a second visit the same day we experienced nothing – the atmosphere was inert. Such clues suggest that the early church builders were very aware of earth energies and knew how to construct a building in order to attract and focus them. To be able to do so would of course greatly enhance the potency of the rituals performed within the structure.

We shall explore earth energies further in Chapter 19 when we discuss leys. These are alignments of ancient sites forming an invisible web of straight lines across the countryside, now surmised by some researchers to be channels for earth energies. Their relevance to the subject of underground structures lies in the many traditions of underground passages which, if we are to believe the tales handed down through the generations, are also widespread throughout Britain. However the courses the passages are said to follow are often impossibly long and difficult,

113

such as beneath a river, and it is exceedingly unlikely that most of these passages ever really existed. It has been suggested that they symbolise or are a distorted memory of leys, or earth energy paths. A ley 4½ miles in length was surveyed in Kent by Paul Devereux, editor of *The Ley Hunter* magazine, and he found that there was a legend of a tunnel connecting Coldrum barrow with Trottiscliffe church, following the line of the ley. The legend also said that there was hidden treasure in the tunnel, a feature also found in other similar tales, which could refer to the power or energy flowing along the ley. Some genuine underground passages have been explored, and they usually appear to have been constructed as sewers, or for a water-supply, or as escape passages from castles, for example Dover Castle (Kent).

Several underground passages were built at Glastonbury (Somerset), and one dug on the orders of Abbot Selwood in about 1470 leads from a medieval inn into the abbey grounds, possibly being intended as a secret access to the abbey. A Mrs Bilbrough who entered this passage earlier this century wrote:

> Off we started on our underground journey down a flight of fearfully steep steps, dark and damp and slippery ... We groped our way to where the far-famed passage was, which had a great stone step at the entrance, and was only three feet in height, so that those who used it must have crawled on their knees, resting at intervals where ledges are cut in the sides for that purpose. Fancy going for a quarter mile like that, when even a few feet of it made my back ache and my limbs quiver all over from the unnatural strained position.

There are also numerous other enigmatic caves and passages in Britain, which were often discovered by accident and the purpose of which remains unknown. Perhaps the strangest is Royston Cave (Hertfordshire), discovered by workmen in 1742 (see 'Places to Visit'). In Nottingham, many passages and chambers have been cut into the Castle Rock, and elsewhere, some of them still accessible. The early inhabitants lived in caves, and 'Nottingham' is a corruption of the Anglo-Saxon *snodenge* (caves) and *ham* (house). Some of the caves at Kinver Edge (Staffordshire) were occupied until this century; London is riddled with underground passages, ancient and modern; and the county of Kent is rich in caves and tunnels, such as the complex system of Chislehurst Caves, which are thought to have been mines. For more information on all these places, and others not mentioned here, see Nigel Pennick's comprehensive and interesting book *The Subterranean Kingdom*.

114

PLACES TO VISIT

Grimes Graves, Norfolk

Location: 5 miles north-west of Thetford, and approached along forest tracks. (TL 817898)

An area of conifer plantations is dotted with craters, nearly 400 of them, the remains of Neolithic flint mines. A shaft up to 40 feet deep led down to galleries, and one shaft can be explored by visitors. An iron ladder reaches down 30 feet to the gallery entrance. The men who worked these mines 5,000 years ago used picks made of deer antlers. Large blocks of stone were taken to the surface to be cut to shape. When the mines were first explored, a statuette was found, a small representation of the Earth Mother, together with a phallus made of chalk, a pile of flints and some antler picks. This has been interpreted as an offering to the goddess in the hope that she would increase the supply of flint.

Carn Euny fogou, Cornwall

Location: 4 miles west-south-west of Penzance, and reached along narrow lanes south-west of Sancreed. (SW 403288)

The fogou is the most impressive structure at Carn Euny Iron Age settlement. It is about 65 feet in length, with a low 'creep'

The circular chamber by Carn Euny fogou seen from inside, looking back towards its entrance.

passage at one end. By the entrance is a circular chamber which originally had a corbelled roof; no other fogou is known which had a chamber of this kind. The fogou had drains and a paved floor, and is thought to have been built for storage purposes, though the inner chamber could equally well have been used as a means of concentrating earth energies, similar to the church crypts described earlier, and may conceivably have been used for shamanistic initiatory practices. There is also a fogou at Chysauster settlement not far away, but it is not nearly so well preserved.

Halligye fogou, Cornwall

Location: 8 miles north-north-east of the Lizard Point. An O.S. map will be needed to locate this fogou. Take the lane leading north-east from Garras, then a lane leading east. After half a mile park and walk uphill across a field to the fogou, which is near a farm. A torch will be needed. (SW 712238)

Halligye fogou.

This fogou survives at the site of a long-gone fortified settlement or farmstead, dating from the period 100 BC to the third century AD. The passage is around 54 feet long, and a cross-passage at the eastern end forms a T-shape. The original entrance at the north led into the ditch of the fortifications, but it is now blocked and the fogou is entered through a hole made in the nineteenth century. This fogou probably served a dual role of storage and refuge; a ridge in the floor is thought to have been placed there to cause uninvited visitors to stumble.

Culsh souterrain, Aberdeen/Grampian Region

Location: 1½ miles north-east of Tarland, beside Culsh Farm and the B9119. A torch will be needed. (NJ 505055)

Dating from the late Iron Age, this is a well preserved souterrain which is easily accessible. The curved entrance passage leads into a spacious dry chamber high enough to allow you to stand upright, which is unusual in souterrains.

Souterrains in County Louth

Location of Kilcurley souterrain: 2 miles west of Dundalk. (J 01 07)

Several good examples of Irish souterrains can be visited in County Louth, notably the Kilcurley/Kilkerley souterrain (also known as Donaghmore souterrain) which is very elaborate, with five passages totalling almost 250 feet in length. There are air vents to provide an air supply, and it is thought that this and similar elaborate souterrains were used as refuges from cattle-raiders, perhaps the Norsemen who were active in this part of the country, which could explain why there are so many souterrains in a relatively small area.

Also worth seeing are the souterrains at Drumad (close to the Newry–Dundalk road) and Stickillin, and the very late, thirteenth century, examples at Ballybarrack, built to provide refuge against invading Normans. Away from County Louth, there are fine souterrains elsewhere in Ireland, including Drumena (County Down), among the ruins of the stone fort; Dunbeg (County Kerry), inside the promontory fort; Glencolumbkille (County Donegal), in front of the Protestant church; Killala (County Mayo), in the graveyard near the round tower.

Repton church crypt, Derbyshire

Location: Repton is 7 miles south of Derby and the church is in the centre of the village. (SK 303272)

There has been a Christian settlement at Repton since the seventh century, with a monastery which was demolished by the Danes in the ninth century. The church is dedicated to St Wystan, a king who was murdered at 'Wistanstowe' (possibly Wistow, Leicestershire) and buried at Repton, which later became a place of pilgrimage. The chancel and crypt of the present church are all that survive of the tenth-century Anglo-Saxon church; St Wystan was probably buried in the crypt along with other Mercian kings. It is thought that the crypt was built for this purpose, but when it began to be visited by large numbers of pilgrims a new flight of stairs was added to allow them to enter more easily.

Repton church crypt.

Royston Cave, Hertfordshire

Some of the carvings to be seen on the walls of Royston Cave.

Location: In Royston town centre, reached by a tunnel whose entrance is on the A505 (Baldock Street). Open to visitors periodically; enquire locally. (TL 357407)

After its accidental discovery in 1742 this bottle-shaped cave about 28 feet deep became the subject of much speculation. Nothing was found inside, but the walls are covered with carvings, Christian and pagan imagery intermingled. No one knows when or why the cave was made, and the Romans, Saxons and Knights Templar have all been suggested as its originators. It may originally have been a Roman or Saxon dene-hole, or chalk pit, which was later converted into a hermitage in the thirteenth or fourteenth century.

119

10. *The Roman legacy*

In 55 BC when the Roman leader Julius Caesar first landed his troops on the shores of Britain there were few substantial buildings in the land. About AD 450, when the last troops were returning to Rome, they left many military and civilian structures behind them, and these remains are now among the most impressive ancient monuments to be seen here today. Most of the remains are in England, with a few in Wales and Scotland, and none in Ireland. The Romans did not succeed in subduing the whole of Britain and Ireland, despite their apparent military superiority. The native population fought boldly against the invading forces during the years 55 BC to AD 200. This 250-year period of anti-Roman violence indicates that it took a very long time for the Romans to gain some sort of control and to live in relative harmony with the natives. For years after the original invasions there were revolts against the Roman presence. In the early years some very bloody battles were fought. In AD 60-1, 70,000 inhabitants of Colchester, London and St Albans were massacred, as a result of Boudicca's rebellion. In AD 83-4 30,000 Caledonians were killed at the Battle of Mons Graupius in Scotland.

Such events as these explain why so much of the surviving Roman architecture is military. The army's temporary 'marching camps' consisted of earth ramparts and so are less impressive than the permanent forts built of stone. The best examples of these are well worth visiting – see Chesters, Housesteads and Hardknott in 'Places to Visit'. The buildings which can be seen at such forts usually include headquarters buildings, bathhouses, barrack-blocks, granaries and latrines. During the later years of their occupation the Romans had to defend south-east England against raids by Saxon pirates, and to this end built a series of massive 'Saxon shore forts' of which the best examples are Pevensey (East Sussex), Portchester (Hampshire), Richborough and Burgh Castle (the last two described in 'Places to Visit').

One lasting Roman legacy which we now take for granted is the existence of towns – before the Roman occupation there were no towns in Britain. A great many of our towns and cities were founded by the Romans and these often have impressive Roman remains hidden away among the dual-carriageways and factories; other Roman towns have shrunk back to village size, as for example Wroxeter (Shropshire – see 'Places to Visit'), which was the Roman city of Viroconium covering 200 acres and the fourth largest town in Roman Britain. One advantage of a failure to grow has been that the Roman remains have not been obliterated by more modern buildings, and at Wroxeter a great deal of the town is now covered by open fields. This greatly facilitates archaeological excavation, and a long-term programme of excavation has been in progress there since 1955, though digging takes place for only six weeks in the summer. In thirty years, only one acre has been completely excavated, though other parts have been partially excavated. As Dr Graham Webster, archaeologist in charge of the project, commented: 'At the rate we are going, it would take at least 6,000 years to dig the whole of the city. This gives an indication of its size and complexities, and also its vast potential for historical information.'

Elsewhere in Britain, a great variety of public buildings has already been excavated and can be visited, such as the theatre at St Albans (Hertfordshire), the town-houses at Canterbury (Kent) and Dorchester (Dorset), the amphitheatre at Maumbury Rings, Dorchester (Dorset), the Roman baths at Bath (Avon), the vaults below the now-lost Temple of Claudius at Colchester (Essex), the three gateways at Lincoln, the bathhouse at Wroxeter (Shropshire), the Jewry Wall, part of an exercise-hall, at Leicester, the bath-house at Wall (Staffordshire), the amphitheatre at Chester, and the magnificent town-wall at Caerwent (Gwent). The best-known Roman remains are the villas, many of which have very well preserved mosaic floors. Here lived the wealthiest Romans – officials, landowners, even kings. The palace at Fishbourne (West Sussex) was unparalleled in Britain in the first century AD, 10 acres of elaborately decorated rooms, halls, colonnades, which is thought to have been the home of King Cogidubnus. Other villas worth seeing include Bignor (West Sussex), Lullingstone (Kent), Rockbourne (Hampshire), Brading, Newport and Combley (all on the Isle of Wight), Littlecote Park (Wiltshire), King's Weston (Avon), Great Witcombe and Chedworth (Gloucestershire), and North Leigh (Oxfordshire).

Archaeological excavations in progress at Wroxeter; on the right are the 'Old Work', part of the baths exercise-hall, and an observation platform for visitors.

The Romans are also famous, of course, for their long, straight roads, whose course can be traced today along modern roads which still bear the Roman names, such as Fosse Way, Watling Street and Ermine Street. More interesting are the small sections of road where the original Roman surface can still be seen. On Blackstone Edge near Rochdale (Greater Manchester) a stretch of road is still paved with large stone setts (rectangular blocks), while at Holtye (East Sussex) a stretch of Roman road metalled with iron slag has been preserved. The best length of Roman road still to be seen is on Wheeldale Moor (North Yorkshire), where it is known as Wade's Causeway from the folklore belief that it was built by the giant Wade. The road runs for $1\frac{1}{4}$ miles across open moorland, and the large stones which are now visible would have originally been covered by gravel to make a smoother surface. Some kerb-stones and drainage culverts can also be seen.

From this brief description of the legacy of Roman Britain it will be understood that when the Romans came they brought with them an entirely new way of civilised life such as had never been seen before by the majority of the native peoples. We of the twentieth century can identify with the domestic aspects of

122

the Romans' lives, as in many respects our own way of life is very similar. But when we come to examine their religious practices, we find them almost as incomprehensible as the practices of the people of the Iron, Bronze and New Stone Ages before them. But a great deal more is known about the Roman religions than about those of earlier ages, for they left behind many stone monuments such as altars and tombstones, which often carry lengthy inscriptions. These show that a wide range of deities was worshipped, which ones often depending on the

Wade's Causeway, a stretch of Roman road on the North York Moors.

practices of the part of the world where the group of people concerned originated. The Roman armies and their families were drawn from many different nations, each with their own religious customs.

When the Romans first entered Britain they faced great opposition from, among others, the Druids, who had both religious and political influence in the Celtic areas of the west. The Romans therefore did all they could to overcome the Druids, and probably succeeded in wiping them out, or at least in making any surviving leaders powerless. However, as time went on, some of the native gods and goddesses were absorbed into the Roman pantheon, so that there came a time when the Romans did not see anything strange in the worship of deities with Celtic origins. A fertility cult centred on the mother goddesses was popular and widespread, for example, and at Benwell, on Hadrian's Wall, a Roman altar was erected to a local Celtic deity, Antenociticus. There are many other examples of this adoption of deities from other religions. Christianity, too, had been adopted in some areas by the third and fourth centuries, after much persecution of Christians in earlier centuries, such as the martyrdom of St Alban. Eventually Christianity became an accepted state religion. Christian symbols like the chi-rho have been found on artefacts such as the lead tanks found at Icklingham (Suffolk) and thought to have been used for baptism. Traces of small Christian churches from the Roman period have also been found, as at Silchester (Hampshire).

It follows that from the Roman period we have a strange mixture of religious sites – temples devoted to the worship of eastern deities such as Mithras, a Persian god (see the Mithraeum at Carrawburgh in 'Places to Visit'), temples where Celtic practices were followed, usually located at sites considered sacred to the old religion, such as hillforts (the foundations of such a temple can still be seen on top of Maiden Castle, Dorset), and early Christian churches such as the one at Silchester already mentioned. By the time the Romans were forced to relax their hold on Britain, around AD 400, when troops had to be withdrawn in order to defend Italy, the Christian religion had gained greatly in popularity. In later centuries it continued to spread throughout Britain and Ireland, though not without considerable resistance from those who preferred to practise their age-old pagan religions, and in the next chapter we shall continue to trace the gradual establishment of Christianity in Britain.

124

PLACES TO VISIT

Hadrian's Wall, stretching across northern England from Cumbria in the west to Newcastle in the east

Location: The wall is well preserved along much of its length. Particularly noteworthy are the stretches at Housesteads (described elsewhere in 'Places to Visit') and Walltown Crags north-west of Haltwhistle (Northumberland). (Walltown Crags: NY 6766)

'... the great wall of Hadrian is not just the most exciting relic of the Roman occupation of Britain, but perhaps the largest and most remarkable building-programme ever undertaken in these islands at any time.' Thus Roger J. A. Wilson in his *Guide to the Roman Remains in Britain* sums up the importance of this impressive 73½-mile frontier. It is still impressive today, despite centuries of erosion: when originally built it was 8–10 feet wide and around 20 feet high, with a 9-foot ditch on the north side

Hadrian's Wall on Walltown Crags (Northumberland).

and a vallum (earthworks) 120 feet across on the southern side. Regularly along the length of the wall were turrets and milecastles (small forts with gates), and there were sixteen large forts close by with a full complement of soldiers ready for action, probably 12,000 men in all.

Construction of the wall was begun in AD 122 and finished by 128. During the succeeding 300 years it was alternately abandoned or damaged during attacks and then restored several times, but the mere fact of its being necessary to maintain such a wall indicates the degree of hostility which the Romans faced. Roger Wilson suggests that it was built to separate the Brigantes of north England from the tribes of southern Scotland, to prevent their getting together in a joint uprising against the Romans. That it was not totally successful in keeping the local tribes quiescent is shown by the evidence of destruction at various times.

Housesteads fort on Hadrian's Wall, Northumberland

Location: 4 miles north-west of Haydon Bridge, reached along the B6318. (NY 7968)

The north gate of Housesteads fort on Hadrian's Wall, which can be seen continuing into the distance.

Vercovicium, as it was known to the Romans, is the most impressive and most popular of the forts along Hadrian's Wall.

As the photograph shows, it is high up in wild, open country, and actually adjoins the wall; to the west is a particularly fine stretch. Inside the rectangular fort, which in the third century housed around 1,000 Belgian soldiers, the foundations of a number of buildings are visible, including barrack-blocks, the commandant's house, the headquarters building, a hospital, a granary, and, most interesting of all, the best-preserved Roman latrine in Britain.

Chesters fort (Cilurnum), Northumberland

Location: 4 miles north of Hexham. (NY 9170)

Chesters originally lay across Hadrian's Wall, but this is now difficult to appreciate, as the wall is scarcely visible at this point. The ruins of the fort are very fine, second only to Housesteads. Among the buildings which can be traced are a barrack-block, gateways, the commandant's private bath-suite with the hypocaust still visible, the headquarters building, a strong-room below ground level, and various other buildings. Most impressive, however, is the bath-house close to the river, some of the walls still standing 10 feet high. Niches used as clothes lockers have been identified; also a latrine and a stoke-hole.

Temple of Mithras, Carrawburgh, Northumberland

Location: 4 miles north of Haydon Bridge, alongside the B6318. (NY 8571)

The temple is beside the earthworks which were once the fort of Brocolitia. The building was extended and repaired during its period of use, which was roughly a hundred years from *c.* AD 200. Inside are copies of the altars and sculptures found there: a statuette of the mother goddess and three altars standing by the end wall (the originals are in the museum at Newcastle). It is ruins like this which really stir the imagination, and make us realise how different were the ways of the Romans from what is familiar to us today, with regard to religious practices. Mithras was a Persian god of light, and the cult of Mithras was popular in military circles in the third and fourth centuries. The Mithraeum, or temple of Mithras, was an artificial cave, symbolising the rock from which Mithras was born. One of his exploits was the killing of a wild bull, which caused the release of blessings upon the earth, and the temples would have contained a sculp-

Temple of Mithras, Carrawburgh.

ture depicting this event. The ceremonies were held in semi-darkness, lit by torches and fires burning on the altars. There is evidence that the temples of Mithras in Britain were desecrated and the sculptures damaged or concealed early in the fourth century, probably by Christians who are known to have been hostile to the cult of Mithras elsewhere in the Roman Empire.

Hardknott fort, Cumbria

Location: On the west side of Hardknott Pass, 9 miles west of Ambleside. Warning: the road through the pass is extremely hazardous. (NY 2101)

This fort, Mediobogdum, must surely be the most spectacularly sited of any Roman structure, with long views over mountain and valley. It must also have been a very cold place in the winter! The outlines of a number of buildings are preserved, and the encircling wall still stands 8–10 feet high.

Leicester (SK 5804)

Leicester was the Roman town of Ratae Coritanorum, the tribal

128

capital of the Coritani. Although there are no town walls visible, and in fact most of Roman Leicester has long since disappeared, a small site has been preserved near the Saxon church of St Nicholas. Here can be seen a fine stretch of Roman wall 30 feet high, called the Jewry Wall. It was part of the baths exercise-hall, similar to the Old Work at Wroxeter (described elsewhere in this chapter). The other visible remains are a public bath-house and part of a town house. There is a museum adjoining the site, which houses many fine Roman artefacts from the area, including painted wall-plaster and mosaics.

The Lunt fort, Warwickshire

Location: At Baginton, 2 miles south of Coventry. (SP 344752)

This early fort was occupied for only a short while in the first century AD, and is now of interest only because of the authentic buildings which have been reconstructed here during the last twenty years. Most impressive is the eastern gateway, constructed of earthworks with timber gate-tower and rampart-walkway. Inside the fort a timber granary has been built, which is used as a museum. Also to be seen are the layout of the headquarters building, and a circular area where horses and cavalrymen may have trained, for this fort seems to have been an army training-ground.

Wroxeter, Shropshire

Location: 5 miles south-east of Shrewsbury. (SJ 5608)

Originally a military fortress, Wroxeter became Viroconium Cornoviorum, the capital of the Cornovii tribe and the fourth largest town in Roman Britain. The town began to grow during the first century AD, and may have been occupied into the sixth century. The visible remains are today dominated by the Old Work, a fine stretch of wall which was part of the baths exercise-hall, as at Leicester. The large hole was for double doors. Excavations in the area of the exercise-hall are still continuing. On the other side are the remains of the public baths. The only visible Roman swimming-bath in Britain can also be seen – it was open to the sky and perhaps for this reason was not popular: it was soon turned into a rubbish pit! A market-hall and latrine have also been uncovered, and a row of columns which were part of a portico along the side of the

129

forum, but much of Wroxeter still lies hidden beneath the surrounding fields. Carvings and other finds can be seen in the museum.

Caerleon, Gwent

Location: Near the south coast of Wales, just to the north-east of Newport. (ST 3490)

Caerleon, or Isca, is probably the most impressive Roman site in Wales, even though only small parts of the great 50-acre fortress are now visible. These are the bath-house (near the Bull Inn), two cook-houses, a latrine, and barrack-blocks. Not far away from these is the magnificent amphitheatre, the only one completely excavated. It dates from AD 80 and was probably used for military exercises rather than gladiatorial contests. Many of the finds are housed in the local museum.

Burgh Castle, Norfolk

Location: Beside the River Waveney, 3 miles west of Gorleston on Sea. (TG 4704)

Burgh Castle or Gariannonum was one of the forts built as a defence against the raids of Saxon pirates in the third century. The leaning walls still stand 8 feet thick and 15 feet high, though the western wall no longer survives.

Richborough fort, Kent

Location: 1 mile north of Sandwich. (TR 3260)

During the first century Richborough (or Rutupiae) was Roman Britain's chief port. It now stands 2 miles inland, but it was originally on a small peninsula joined to the mainland. Inside can be seen the slight remains of a double ditch dug in AD 43 by the invading Roman army – these ditches are the earliest Roman remains in Britain. The larger triple ditches were dug in the third century. Richborough is a complex site, with many interesting features surviving, at least in fragments, such as the heap of rubble which was once an arch nearly 90 feet high. The walls of the Saxon shore fort were built towards the end of the third century, and stood 30 feet high – sections are still well preserved. Also in the fort is the groundplan of a small Saxon church; the foundations of an earlier Christian church, dating from the Roman period, are no longer visible.

Pharos at Dover, Kent

Location: In the grounds of Dover Castle. (TR 326418)

A 'pharos' was a lighthouse, and this fine example adjoining St Mary's church is the only one surviving in Britain. Originally it would have stood about 80 feet high; today it is only 60 feet high, and the top third of that is medieval work. It was probably built during the second century, and a fire lit on the top would have guided ships in the Channel. The slight remains of a second lighthouse in Dover have been found on the Western Heights.

Dover Pharos.

11. *Early Christian sacred sites*

The Christians were already active in Britain in the early centuries AD, and as we saw in the previous chapter, after early persecutions Christianity eventually became an acceptable state religion during the Roman period. However, after the departure of the Romans, the Anglo-Saxons became dominant in England, especially in the east and south, and they were pagans. The followers of Christ made little headway in promoting their religion, and the country again became largely pagan. St Augustine arrived from Rome in 597 to rekindle the flame of Christianity, and during the seventh century stone churches began to be built, fragments of which survive in a few present-day churches, as at Brixworth (see 'Places to Visit'). Over the succeeding four centuries many fine churches were built, and some of them have survived without very many changes, so that the Saxon features can still be fully appreciated. When considered on their own terms, unspoilt Saxon churches are as impressive as any of the great architecture of later centuries.

In Wales during this same period, and similarly in the south-western peninsula of England, religion took a very different course. There was no Saxon influence, and Christianity came in from the west, brought by monks from Ireland and Brittany. They settled in the valleys, built tiny oratories and chapels, and preached the gospel to the natives close by, the gradual spread of their individual cults being traced today by the surviving church dedications. Very few buildings have survived from those early days, but in Wales alone there are at least 400 stone monuments from the fifth to the twelfth centuries which carry Christian inscriptions (see Chapter 7). Christianity also spread from the west into Scotland, carried by saints like St Columba, who went from Ireland to Iona in 563, where he founded a monastery. He carried the faith inland, and into the land of the Picts, and died in 597, the year that St Augustine entered England to begin the conversion of the pagan Saxons.

A fine example of Saxon architecture, the late tenth-century tower of Earl's Barton church (Northamptonshire).

132

With the arrival of the Normans in England in the late eleventh century, great changes affected all aspects of life, including religion. The Saxon style of church architecture gave way to the Norman, rich and ornate where the Saxon had been plain and spare – the visible change was from austerity to flamboyance. Decorative carving abounded in Norman churches, and many examples survive. Often found among them are themes which hark back to pre-Christian religions, fertility symbols especially, and the frequency with which such themes occur suggests that paganism was still widely practised and that pagan concepts were incorporated into the church ritual by the early clergy. This is certainly a possibility. The Christian conversion of Britain was achieved neither rapidly nor smoothly, and in many rural areas the people must have continued their age-old practices long after the area was nominally Christian. Edicts were often issued by religious officials in the early centuries to try and stamp out lingering paganism. So the appearance in Christian churches of carvings suggestive of pagan beliefs need not seem anachronistic. The practice of incorporating such carvings into the church fabric also continued into later centuries, but by that time the direct link with paganism would have gone, and the symbols would have had their pagan energies exorcised by long Christian usage. They were probably seen in later centuries as a form of good luck charm, the weird and sometimes frightening faces being thought to keep evil spirits at bay.

Exorcism may have been the motive of the missionaries who built Christian churches on sites previously sacred to the pagans. There are undoubtedly many examples of churches being built at such sites. We have already seen Rudston church built close to a standing stone (see Chapter 4), and here we see Midmar church standing cheek by jowl with a Bronze Age recumbent stone circle. In 'Places to Visit' we describe the standing stone by the porch of Llanwrthwl church; there is a smaller standing stone by the porch of Maentwrog church (Gwynedd) and at Ysbyty Cynfyn church (Dyfed) several standing stones, possibly the remains of a stone circle, are incorporated into the churchyard wall, suggesting that the church was built within an existing circle. Other churches stand inside hillforts, as at Cholesbury (Buckinghamshire), or inside henges, as at Knowlton (Dorset), while others were built on top of burial mounds, as in Jersey where two medieval chapels were constructed on the Neolithic burial mound of La Hougue Bie. Circular churchyards are often found (for example at Old Radnor,

*Midmar church
(Aberdeen/Grampian Region).*

Powys), and are suggestive of prehistoric sacred sites, but raised churchyards are not necessarily evidence of prehistoric burial mounds – continuous use of a graveyard for burials over the centuries will tend to raise the level of the ground (although it cannot raise the level of the church foundations).

Nevertheless, there is plenty of evidence that Christian churches were often established on previously pagan sacred sites. The reason behind this is not so clear. Perhaps the early Christians appreciated the necessity of a continuity of religious practice and understood that they could gain influence over the population by adapting the sites already sacred rather than by bluntly opposing the established practices. They may also have been skilled in the knowledge of terrestrial energies and focal points and knew that to disrupt the established pattern of energy flow would help neither themselves nor the people they had come to convert. For their part the indigenous population were content that the sacred sites were still in use, and found that their ancient gods could with little difficulty be assimilated into the new religion, appearing sometimes in a new guise as saints or as the mother of Christ.

Many legends have survived which tell of churches being mysteriously moved to another site overnight during construction, suggesting that there was conflict between opposing groups over the sitings. This conflict was possibly between

135

Montgomery Church (Powys) possibly on a ley, see Chapter 19.

Christians who wished to incorporate the practices of the old religion into the new, and those who wished irrevocably to sever all connections with it. Or it may have been concerned with arguments about the best place to site the church in order to make full use of the natural earth energies. Those who have studied earth currents by means of dowsing suggest that a flow of water above or below ground provides a good channel for the flow of earth currents, and by dowsing in old churches they can plot the course of underground water lines which flow in and out of the building at significant points and often form an underground spiral or vortex at a point of especial potency. The experiences of ourselves and others indicate that energy flows and pulses may still move through some older church structures, but this evidence is of course completely subjective. Whatever esoteric principles were used by the early Church fathers in siting their foundations, they do not appear to have been recorded, and today's researchers have barely started to delve into the mysteries contained within these sacred sites.

136

PLACES TO VISIT

Llanwrthwl church, Powys

Location: 3 miles south of Rhayader. (SN 976637)

St Gwrthwl's church is only just over a hundred years old, but
the site is clearly ancient: the church stands on a raised knoll
and there is a large standing stone by the south porch. Inside
the church is an ancient font of eleventh- or twelfth-century
date, a circular bowl on the outside of which are four projecting
heads, perhaps an echo of the Celtic head cult (see Clonfert,
Co. Galway, elsewhere in 'Places to Visit', and also Chapter
13).

Gallarus oratory, County Kerry

Location: 4 miles north-west of Dingle. (Q 39 05)

Boat-shaped oratories (small churches) were widely built in
Ireland in early Christian times, and the one which has survived
at Gallarus is the finest example known. Because of its perfec-
tion, it is thought to be a late example, possibly twelfth century.
The walls are 3 feet thick, and slope gradually inwards until   *Gallarus oratory.*

they meet. Close to the oratory is a fine cross-pillar with a worn inscription.

St Non's Chapel, Dyfed

Location: Just south of St David's, on the cliffs above St Non's Bay. (SM 751244)

St Non was the mother of St David, and according to legend he was born at this site, probably early in the sixth century. The chapel, of which only low walls now remain, is thought to be a rare example of the earliest church-building in Britain, dating from the seventh or eighth century. There was also a stone circle here, very slight traces of which can still be seen, so it is a truly ancient site; close by is St Non's Well.

Brough of Birsay, Orkney

Location: 6 miles north of Stromness, on a tidal islet reached along a track. (NY 239285)

This site is thought to have been first occupied in the seventh or early eighth century, and evidence of a small Celtic church has been found under the ruins of the Norse church which are on the site today. Also there was an earlier graveyard beneath the Norse graveyard, and fragments of a wall similar to those found at Celtic monasteries have also been found. A broken Pictish stone, an early cross and a fragment of stone with an Ogham inscription are additional finds.

Many immigrants from Scandinavia came and settled in northern Scotland in the early centuries, and the church here was built in the mid-eleventh century by Earl Thorfinn the Mighty, who settled here after years of raiding. A grave thought to be his was found in the nave of the church, and also another grave possibly that of St Magnus. Close by is another building, probably a twelfth-century bishop's palace. The foundations of a group of Norse houses were also found, one of them likely to have been the home of Earl Thorfinn the Mighty.

Clynnog Fawr church, Gwynedd

Location: At the north end of the Lleyn Peninsula, astride the coast road A499; 10 miles north-north-east of Pwllheli. (SH 414497)

138

The first church here was founded by St Beuno *c.* 616, though the present fine building dates back only as far as the early sixteenth century. Nevertheless Clynnog Fawr is worth visiting for its associations, as a thriving cult of St Beuno grew up here. During restoration work in 1913 the foundations of an older building were found, which may have been part of St Beuno's original church. Adjoining the present church is St Beuno's Chapel, which housed the shrine or tomb of the saint, unfortunately destroyed by fire in 1856. Miracles were said to happen at the shrine, and sick people came for cures. Not far from the church, along the main road, St Beuno's Well is still in existence, where the sick would bathe in hopes of being cured.

Saxon chapel at Bradford-on-Avon, Wiltshire

Location: The town is 6 miles south-east of Bath, and the chapel is opposite Holy Trinity church. (ST 824609)

Until the mid-nineteenth century the existence of this well-preserved Saxon building was unknown, as it was used as a cottage and a school and its true nature was disguised. It is

Saxon chapel at Bradford-on-Avon.

thought to date from the tenth century, and was possibly built to house the body of St Aldhelm, Bishop of Malmesbury. It is an intriguing and atmospheric building, its shape tall and narrow and thus typically Saxon. High up above the chancel arch are some fine carved angels.

Saxon church at Brixworth, Northamptonshire

Location: 6 miles north of Northampton. (SP 747713)

The date when this fine church was built is not known, but it was certainly early, perhaps as early as the seventh century. It may have been the church for a monastery at this site. Only the nave survives of the earliest church, the building having been enlarged and elaborated in the eighth and ninth centuries. A crypt was added in the ninth century, and the tower was possibly built in the same century, the external stair turret being added in the eleventh. The round heads of the external nave arches are made from Roman tiles, Roman materials often being reused in this way. The conservation of old buildings was

Saxon church at Brixworth.

unthought of in earlier centuries than our own, and it is remarkable that any have actually survived.

Saxon church at Breamore, Hampshire

Location: Breamore is 6 miles south of Salisbury, the church being to the north of the village, not far from Breamore House. (SU 153188)

This Saxon church, which probably dates from the late tenth century, is larger than most, perhaps because it was a minster with a royal patron. Apart from the sturdy unspoiled building, the most interesting Saxon feature is the inscription over a doorway inside the church. It is unique, being in an early script which experts date to no later than 1020.

Saxon church at Stow, Lincolnshire

Location: 8 miles north-west of Lincoln. (SK 882819)

This magnificent church dwarfs the small village of Stow; its large size was due to its being the mother church of the area of Lindsey. The first church at Stow was founded in 674 by Ecgfrith, king of Northumbria, at the place where, according to legend, his wife Queen Etheldreda's walking stick grew overnight into a large ash tree. Nothing remains of that first church

Saxon church at Stow.

(unless some fire-damaged stones were part of it; it was destroyed by the Danes in 870), the present building probably dating from the eleventh century.

Much of the present church is Norman, but the fine central crossing arches are Anglo-Saxon, the tallest and widest to have survived. The first view of this great interior is literally breathtaking, an experience not to be missed. The church also has other features of interest, including some good Norman work, a Norman or Early English font carved with a green man and a winged serpent, and a twelfth- or thirteenth-century fresco of St Thomas à Becket.

Clonfert cathedral, County Galway

Location: 9 miles south-east of Ballinasloe. (M 96 21)

The elaborately carved west doorway of St Brendan's cathedral

Clonfert cathedral.

dates from the early thirteenth century, and is 'the finest surviving achievement of Irish Romanesque sculpture and design' (Anthony Weir). Look closely at the six orders of carving round the top of the door and you will see grinning animals, dog-like horse heads, foliage, interlace, and geometrical designs. The unique pointed design above the doorway is topped by a pair of ape heads. Inside the triangle are many human heads, which remind us strongly of the Celtic custom of displaying the severed heads of defeated enemies, this practice being the basis of a widespread head cult, traces of which survive to the present day (for more about the head cult see Chapter 13). This impressive doorway is an eerie yet compelling sight, growing ever more impressive the longer it is studied.

Norman church at Tickencote, Leicestershire

Location: Near the A1, 2½ miles north-west of Stamford. (SK 900095)

Of the many excellent examples of Norman work still to be seen in England, we have chosen to illustrate the extraordinary

Norman church at Tickencote.

chancel arch at Tickencote, which demonstrates the Norman church-builders' love of decoration. As at Clonfert (illustrated elsewhere), there are six orders of carving, and the designs used include beaked heads, grotesques, chevrons and other shapes, and a green man (see Crowcombe, Somerset, following in 'Places to Visit'). The remainder of the church is also of interest, but especially the font which dates from around 1200, and the vaulting in the chancel, which is unique in Norman England, and part of which can just be glimpsed in the photograph.

Bench-end carvings in Crowcombe church, Somerset

Location: In the Quantock Hills, 9 miles north-west of Taunton. (ST 141367)

The green men to be seen on the bench-ends inside Crowcombe church are a late (sixteenth century) and elaborate version of

Bench-end carving in Crowcombe church.

the image seen in many other churches, usually carved in stone and often hidden away. With foliage sprouting from their heads, usually but not always from the mouth, the 'green man' or 'Jack-in-the-Green' seems to symbolise the renewal of life in spring, or the spirit of nature. There may also be a link with the Celtic head cult, as the green man always lacks a body. We have discussed these strange and often eerie carvings, and illustrated other fine examples, in our earlier book *Earth Rites*.

12. Giants on the hills

The hill-figures of southern England are among the most enigmatic monuments which remain from past ages. Of the oldest of them, little is known. Their age, the reasons for their cutting, and the people who cut them, all are a mystery and are likely to remain so. The figures are formed by cutting off the top turf and revealing the white chalk below. The Uffington White Horse (Oxfordshire) is certainly the oldest and most enigmatic of these figures. Cut into the northern slope of the downs near Swindon, it faces north-west and under favourable conditions can be seen from 15 to 20 miles away across the Vale of the White Horse, but due to the slope of the hillside it cannot be clearly seen from below, and the best view of it is from the air. The figure does not trace the conventional outlines of a horse, but what at first might be thought to be a crude and unskilled attempt can on closer study be seen as an imaginative free-flowing interpretation, embodying the feeling of speed and movement of a horse and more akin to twentieth-century artistry than the prosaic delineations of other much more recent hill-horses. Similar stylised animals appear on coins and buckets of the Iron Age and the Uffington horse is provisionally dated at 100 BC. But is it really a horse? The 'beaked' shape of the jaw has caused much speculation, and suggestions that we should really be talking about the Uffington Dragon. Just below in the valley is a flat-topped mound called Dragon Hill. Legend says that here St George killed a dragon and where its blood spilt the grass has never grown since. Perhaps the 'horse' figure was cut as visual confirmation of this legend.

The Westbury White Horse about 2 miles from Bratton in Wiltshire is also a figure of mystery. The horse you can see today was cut in 1778 by Mr Gee, who was Lord Abingdon's steward. It is a handsome and conventional animal, the sort of beast an estate steward would approve of. But what was posterity losing when Mr Gee set his men to work on the slope of Bratton Down? There was already an older horse there, which

An aerial view of the Uffington White Horse: note Dragon Hill below left, and the bank and ditch of the Iron Age hillfort above right.

146

Dragon Hill, Uffington.

had been surveyed and drawn in 1772, and which was an odd-looking beast with a long, thin body, a long, thin tail with a crescent-shaped end, and one large 'goggle' eye on its forehead. Some researchers said that it was no older than the early years of that century, but others, excited by its odd appearance and the connection of a crescent moon shape to Celtic symbolism, believe that the original horse could be as old as that at Uffington. In both cases there is an Iron Age hillfort on the hilltop above, but we shall never know when the white horse of Westbury first appeared.

Two other hill figures of great antiquity depict not horses but men. Said to be the largest human figure in the world, the Long Man of Wilmington at 231 feet 6 inches tall stands on the edge of the downs near Eastbourne (East Sussex), holding a staff in each of his raised hands. The figure is of unknown origin and little attention was paid to it until 1874 when the outline was marked by bricks. How accurate this was and what details were lost are open questions, as a drawing made in 1779 shows the figure with a rakehead and scythe blade on top of the left and right staffs respectively. The Long Man has at various times been identified as depicting Woden, Thor, or other Norse gods,

148

one of the Greco-Roman gods, Mohammed, or St Paul. Others have seen him as a Stone Age surveyor with measuring rods. But his true identity will probably always remain a secret.

The second ancient hill figure in human form is the Cerne Abbas Giant (Dorset) who at first glance appears to be keeping no secrets from us. This muscular male figure brandishing his huge club and striding across the hillside has long been known as a promoter of fertility, as suggested by his large phallus and testicles, and by the long-held belief that a woman who sleeps for a night on the giant will bear many children. Just above him on the hillside is a small square earthwork where for centuries the maypole was erected and May Day festivities were enjoyed. The figure is thought possibly to be Hercules and has been tentatively dated to Romano-British times, due to the similarity to other carved Hercules figures. The fact that this virile fertility symbol has survived through the ages points to the awe in which the local population held him.

The Whiteleaf Cross in Buckinghamshire is another hill figure of unknown age. On a slope of the Chiltern Hills, it faces over the Vale of Aylesbury, close to the Icknield Way. During the past 200 years its size has gradually increased as successive scourings (i.e. cleaning and tidying the edges) have enlarged the outline and it can be seen from 15 or more miles distant. Various suggestions as to its origin have been made, including a landmark for travellers using the Icknield trackway, an ancient fertility sign that was changed into a cross by early Christians, or a cross originally cut by the monks from nearby Missenden Abbey.

There are other hill figures in England, nearly fifty in all, but few of these are of any great age. Of the many white horses in Wiltshire, most are of recent centuries though some may have been recut on top of older figures now lost. Also lost are the Gogmagog Giants on the ramparts of Wandlebury Camp in Cambridgeshire, possibly dating from AD 300, and the Plymouth Giants who were cut on the Hoe, one being in existence in 1486, the second added some centuries later. There was a red horse (red because of the soil colour) at Tysoe (Warwickshire) until 1798 and some early reports suggest that it may have had similarities to both the Uffington horse and the original Westbury horse, and could have been of ancient origin. These figures are soon overgrown if not regularly scoured clean, and they and possibly many others have disappeared over the centuries, taking with them their now-hidden meanings.

149

Uffington White Horse, Oxfordshire

Location: 11 miles east of Swindon, and south of Uffington village. (SU 302866)

This white chalk figure is cut into the turf on the brow of the hill some 500 feet above the Vale of the White Horse, and is 365 feet from head to tail. Below is a steep combe called The Manger, and nearby is a curious flat-topped mound called Dragon Hill. From below the figure is not clearly seen, being too far up on the slope of the hill. The best views of the complete horse are from some miles away across the valley; or from the air. Its origins and meaning are a complete mystery, though it is generally accepted as being very ancient. The first known record of it is found in the twelfth-century records of Abingdon Abbey, and refers to the previous century when land was held near 'White Horse Hill' by the Abbot. There are a number of other references to it in the following two centuries but it seems to have escaped much notice until the eighteenth-century antiquarians took an interest in it and started a controversy which has continued until the present. Some of them attributed the horse to Saxon times, being cut to commemorate victories either by Hengist or Alfred, but today's archaeologists have noted that the stylised drawing is not like that of the Saxons' prancing horse emblem, which faced left, but is very much like the way the Iron Age Celts of around 100 BC depicted horses and other animals on their artefacts. The Celts were great horsemen and Epona was one of their numerous horse goddesses. The Uffington horse could be a tribute to one of these. But the way in which the neck, back and tail are formed by one continuous sweeping line is also very similar to various Bronze Age rock carvings, and this could place it at an even earlier date.

Because of its sinuous shape and beaky mouth, some doubt that it was meant as a horse at all. Nearby is Dragon Hill where traditionally St George killed the dragon, the bare patch of chalk on top is where its blood was spilt, and no grass will grow there. Was the horse or dragon cut on the hillside to commemorate this daring deed, or was it the emblem or totem animal of the Iron Age people who inhabited the nearby earthwork of Uffington Castle, proclaiming their dominion over the valley below? The only really satisfactory view of it is from overhead, so possibly it was intended as a tribute to the gods who would view it from the heavens.

The white chalk hill figures of southern England are constructed by removing the turf and revealing the white chalk subsoil below. The difficult part is getting the outlines correct so that from a distance the figure looks like what it is meant to depict. The eighteenth and nineteenth century landowners who amused themselves by having white horses cut on their hillsides apparently used a technique involving flags pegged out according to instructions shouted through a megaphone, and this sort of trial and error method is the only obvious way. Once cut, the figure would soon become overgrown if not kept clean and fresh chalk pounded on to the surface, and so the 'scouring' was organised generally every seventh year. The Uffington scouring was done over two days by the people of the surrounding villages. The Lord of the Manor provided food and drink; games, contests and sports took place within the embankments of Uffington Castle; and the area was filled with sideshows, drinking booths and all the fun of the fair. Cheeses were rolled down the steep slope of The Manger, to be chased and caught as prizes, a similar event still taking place annually at Birdlip in Gloucestershire. The regularity of these gatherings lapsed in the second half of the nineteenth century and by the beginning of the twentieth the festivities had ceased.

Such festive gatherings on sacred hilltops with horse and foot races and similar other pastimes occurred at other significant sites in Britain, usually within the earth embankments of a fort, and are doubtless of very ancient origin, as is the cheese-rolling contest. They were just a part of the annual round of rites and customs practised by the ancient people, about which more will be said in Chapter 18.

Westbury White Horse, Wiltshire

Location: On the edge of the downs between Westbury and
   Bratton, and 4½ miles south-east of Trowbridge.
   (ST 900516)

The present white horse of Westbury is only just over 200 years old, having been cut in 1778 as described earlier. The date of origin of the earlier horse has always been uncertain. Its first published mention appears in a book of 1742 by the Reverend Francis Wise who was told that the horse was cut recently within the memory of those living. The horse Wise saw was an odd-looking creature, judging by a drawing of 1772. Facing to the right, as does the Uffington horse, but unlike other later

151

white horses, it had a long, dog-like body, a thin tail with a barbed end, and spindly legs. This unhorselike appearance must have offended Mr Gee who obliterated it by incorporating it into a much larger animal which, with a few alterations over the years, is essentially what we can see today. Antiquarians of the eighteenth century thought that the cutting of the horse was done to commemorate a victory of King Alfred over the Danes in 878, a similar story being attached to the Uffington White Horse, but there is no evidence for these beliefs. By 1872 the horse was neglected and falling into disrepair, and in 1873 a local committee repaired it and edged the figure with large slabs of stone set on edge. Later gratings were fitted to carry off the rain-water which flowed down the steep slope and washed away much of the chalk surface, and in 1936 concrete was added to combat this erosion.

The horse lies on a steep slope of Salisbury Plain below the Iron Age earthwork of Bratton Castle, from whose heights may be seen, in favourable weather, two other Wiltshire white horses, at Cherhill and Alton Barnes some 20 miles away.

Westbury White Horse.

The Cerne Abbas Giant, Dorset

Location: On a hill above Cerne Abbas, which is 5½ miles north of Dorchester. (ST 666017)

The Cerne Giant is cut into the hillside above the village and is 180 feet tall and 44 feet wide at the shoulders. His outline is marked by a trench 2 feet wide and as deep. Brandishing his 120-foot-long club and with his prominently erect phallus he epitomises energy, vitality and fertility. When the figure was made and by whom are unknown. At different times it has been suggested that it represents a Celtic god Belinus, Hercules, or a Saxon prince. It was also said to have been cut by the monks of a local monastery as a joke against their abbot. Though this last suggestion is unlikely to be the answer, the respect for the figure and its maintenance over the centuries by the local people were tolerated if not encouraged by the religious house, which suggests that they had an understanding and sympathy for the figure's essential meaning and significance. The veneration of the phallus as a symbol of fecundity is very ancient and wide-

An aerial view of the Cerne Abbas Giant, also showing (above his head) the small earthwork known as The Trendle, where May festivities were held.

spread and even today there are examples of carved stone phalli to be found in and near churches throughout Europe. Above the giant on the hillside is the small earth-banked enclosure called The Trendle wherein the maypole was erected for the May Day festivities, which were again dedicated to the continuance of fertility.

The Long Man of Wilmington, East Sussex

Location: On the north-facing slope of Windover Hill south of Wilmington, which is itself 3 miles north-west of Eastbourne. (TQ 542034)

This figure, who is also known as the Lanky Man or the Lone Man and even, when overgrown with grass, as the Green Man, is 231 feet 6 inches tall. His staffs are 237 feet 6 inches and 241 feet 6 inches high, and are 115 feet apart. The shape we see today was outlined in pale yellow brick by members of the Sussex Archaeological Trust in 1874 and shows a slim, athletic figure facing the onlooker and holding a long staff in each hand. There is in existence a rough sketch made in 1779 by Sir William Burrell which shows a much stockier figure with bent knees, toes pointing outwards, and holding a rake in the right hand and a scythe in the left. Though this drawing was not done on site and is probably inaccurate in detail, it does indicate that earlier the figure may have looked rather different from what it does today. In fact in earlier centuries it was not easily seen because the trench marking the outline was customarily overgrown and its shape could only be discerned by the strong side light of a rising sun. Perhaps this was the way in which it was meant to be seen – only by those who secretly worshipped whatever deity the Long Man represented.

The age of this figure is completely unknown and its appearance provides even fewer clues than do those of the enigmatic Cerne Abbas Giant or Uffington White Horse. Speculation has attached the names of various humans and deities to the Long Man, including Baldur, Beowulf, Woden, Thor, Varuna, Boötes, Apollo and Mercury, as well as Mohammed and St Paul, those last two because it was a popular belief that the figure of a cock was sometimes faintly visible on the hillside to the right of the figure and they were both associated with that bird. The Long Man has also been identified as a Roman standard bearer and an ancient British surveyor. The Saxon King Harold used the figure of a fighting man as an emblem and some have suggested that the Long Man represents this; others think that he was cut on the hillside by the monks of Wilmington Priory as a sign to pilgrims to indicate a safe lodging for the night. Much more information on the history and possible interpretations of this enigmatic figure can be found in a recent book, *The Wilmington Giant* by Rodney Castleden.

Whether the Long Man was first cut centuries ago by a prehistoric tribe, or on an eighteenth-century whim, we shall probably never know; but he continues to keep watch across the Sussex Downs, and to keep his secrets.

Long Man of Wilmington.

155

13. *Holy wells and water cults*

Evidence for the veneration of water can be found back in prehistoric times. Stone circles and avenues were often located close to a water source, and ritual shafts or wells were dug during the Neolithic period and the Bronze Age. Objects found in these wells may have been offerings to the deity of the well, or of the underworld, into which the well was an entrance. The custom of throwing offerings into wells continued through Roman times, and in fact has never ceased – today people still respond to the impulse to throw coins into 'wishing wells'. Water was of great importance in the Celtic religion, which was an outdoor religion, and in addition to their sacred groves of trees they had sacred rivers, streams, pools and springs. We have already mentioned the Celtic head cult (see Chapter 11), and this seems to have had some connection with sacred pools and springs. The Celts venerated the head as the source of all the attributes they most admired, and they brought home the heads of notable enemies so that these could be displayed to their visitors. They also used carved heads as decorative devices, and they can be seen on all types of Celtic artefacts.

Many Celtic traditions and beliefs never died out but were perpetuated in various ways down the succeeding centuries. Among reminders of the head cult are the carvings of heads which decorate Christian churches, especially in Celtic areas, though for many centuries the carvers have been simply following a tradition without being aware of its gruesome origins. One good example of carved heads, the Clonfert cathedral doorway, was illustrated in Chapter 11. The lore and practices of holy wells also contain various reminders of the head cult. At St Teilo's Well, Llandeilo (Dyfed), the water had to be drunk from the skull of St Teilo, if a cure was to be effected. A similar practice was followed at other wells, but so far as we know none of these skulls has survived to the present day, although that at St Teilo's Well was only lost in this century. Some wells were associated with decapitation stories, in that the water was said

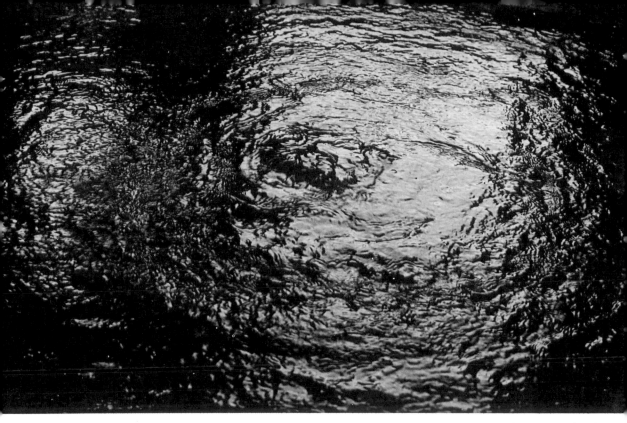

to have started to flow where a severed head fell. In Scotland, the decapitated heads of seven men, killed in revenge for murder, were washed in the water of a well. This event is now commemorated in the name of the well, The Well of the Heads (at Loch Oich, Inverness/Highland Region), and in a monument erected in 1812 which is topped by a hand holding a dirk and seven heads.

Water worship was also clearly an aspect of Roman religious practices. A number of pagan temples were sited close to water, and sometimes special wells were constructed within the temple compound. The best-known example is Coventina's Well at Carrawburgh (Northumberland) which was only a few feet from the Mithraeum described and illustrated in Chapter 10. When excavated the well was found to contain a great variety of objects – stone and bronze heads and a human skull (possible relics of a head cult), models of a horse and a dog, jewellery, pottery, and 14,000 coins (offerings?) and twenty-four altars. The altars were probably hidden in the well when danger threatened. They were in good condition and some were carved with water nymphs and goddesses. That some Roman wells were visited in order to cure illnesses is known from the evidence at Lydney (Gloucestershire) where the Temple of

The heart of St Winefride's Well at Holywell (see 'Places to Visit') where the water swirls up strongly. Many pilgrims still visit this shrine seeking cures.

157

Stone heads project from the eleventh- or twelfth-century font in Llanwrthwl church (Powys), an echo of the Celtic head cult and its association with water.

Nodens and associated buildings were used as a healing centre on quite a large scale. In addition to the temple, there were a square courtyard house, a suite of baths and a long building divided into cubicles, where patients may have spent the night in the hope of being visited by the god. There was also a healing centre at the famous Roman baths in Bath (Avon).

Water worship was still practised widely in Britain and Ireland when Christianity was first introduced, and it must have been evident to the missionaries and religious leaders that this and other pagan practices could not be easily eradicated. Far better, therefore, to adapt them to Christian usage, and this did indeed work very well in the case of the water cult. Many wells were used for Christian baptisms, and small chapels and baptisteries were built close by, these often being replaced later by larger churches. Today many churches still have holy wells near to them, and some are illustrated in 'Places to Visit'. In some places the water from holy wells is still used for baptisms, being fetched to the church specially for this purpose. But although the wells were now Christianised, and dedicated to Christian saints, the simple people who were accustomed to visit them had no desire to change their old ways, and so they continued to practise rituals whose origins lay deep in prehistory. They could discern no essential difference between the pagan deities and the Christian saints.

The rituals were usually performed in an attempt to cure an ailment, for this is the most important reason why holy wells

158

continued to be visited through the centuries. Many wells were said to cure all illnesses, but others were good for only specific ailments, eye troubles being one of the commonest. Others often mentioned include childhood ailments like rickets and whooping cough, infertility, rheumatic ailments, skin complaints, indigestion, deafness, headache, toothache, madness – in fact all the afflictions suffered by mankind. The rituals which had to be performed were sometimes quite time-consuming and complex, but they usually ended with the pilgrim leaving an offering, often a pin, a pebble, or a piece of clothing fastened to a tree or bush. No one is absolutely sure of the significance of the offerings, whether they represented a gift to the saint or deity, or whether the pilgrim expected that his disease would be transferred to the rag which he fastened to a nearby bush, and that as the rag rotted away, so too would his affliction disappear. Today people still leave offerings at holy wells (see the Cloutie Well in 'Places to Visit'), but usually from custom and not with any understanding of what they are doing.

Because of the important role they played in people's lives over the centuries, holy wells have accumulated a rich body of folklore, especially relating to how the wells came into existence. Some were formed in answer to the prayers of a saint who needed water; sometimes water flowed where the saint's staff struck the ground. We have already mentioned the springs which appeared where severed heads fell. Sometimes a spring appeared where a dead body was briefly laid. Two Herefordshire wells resulted from the death of Ethelbert, king of East Anglia, in the eighth century. He was first buried at Marden, and a spring began to flow in the empty grave when the body was removed to Hereford. The well can still be seen, inside the church. The body was briefly rested not far from the place where Hereford Cathedral now stands, and there a second spring flowed. This no longer exists, but a plaque marks the spot. The cathedral stands on the site of a shrine erected to the memory of the dead king in 795 by King Offa of Mercia, who had been responsible for Ethelbert's death.

The folklore of holy wells also includes tales about the water divinities who were venerated. The divinities could take a variety of forms, including ghostly women in white, fairies, mermaids, and also animal forms, usually fishes or eels. A large number of wells contained one or two sacred fishes or eels, which were treated with great respect by the people who visited the wells. They would watch the movements of the fish or eel, and by these movements they could predict future events, usually the course of a love affair, or the outcome of an illness. Whatever form the divinity took, it was greatly revered by the pilgrims as embodying the spirit of the well, and was to be placated and not angered, hence the importance of the rituals and the leaving of offerings.

At the height of their popularity there were literally thousands of holy wells being actively used throughout England, Wales, Scotland and Ireland. Many survive to this day, but except for Ireland and some of the more remote areas of Scotland, they are rarely visited by pilgrims, but rather by people fascinated by their history. Too many holy wells have been lost by neglect, and with the hope of arousing people's interest in this intriguing aspect of Britain's heritage, we have recently compiled a book on them, *Sacred Waters: Holy Wells and Water Lore in Britain and Ireland.* We included a gazetteer of two hundred wells still surviving, from which we have selected just a few of the best preserved and most atmospheric for 'Places to Visit'.

This carefully carved inscription of 150 years ago testifies to the widespread fame of St Winefride's Well.

PLACES TO VISIT

St Winefride's Well, Holywell, Clwyd

Location: In the town of Holywell, below the church and beside
the B5121. (SJ 185763)

St Winefride's is one of the few holy wells in Britain which is
still visited by people seeking cures. It is a Catholic shrine, with
candles constantly burning by the water. An elaborate stone
chapel stands over the well, whose fast-bubbling water fills a
large open-air bathing pool. According to legend, a spring
began to flow here at the spot where St Winefride's head fell,
when she was attacked by a frustrated suitor. Fortunately for St
Winefride, St Beuno was close at hand. He replaced her head on
her neck, and she made a full recovery, except for a thin line
round her neck. Her chapel and well have been visited for
centuries by pilgrims of all ranks, from the humblest peasant to
kings and queens.

St Withburga's Well, East Dereham, Norfolk

Location: In the churchyard, close to St Nicholas's church.
(TF 986134)

This is a good example of a holy well close to a church. Others
described here are at Holywell, Stoke Edith, Partrishow, Penmon, Binsey and Stevington, more than half of the holy wells in
'Places to Visit', which shows how frequently they are found
close to churches.

St Withburga's Well marks the spot where the saint's body
was buried before being stolen and taken away to Ely Cathedral
in 974. A chapel was built over the well, the slight walls of
which can still be seen, but there is no trace now of the
eighteenth-century bath-house.

Holy well at St Cleer, Cornwall

Location: St Cleer is 2 miles north of Liskeard, and the well is
beside a road in the village. (SX 249683)

Of the English counties, Cornwall is by far the richest in holy
wells, many of which have been preserved. The well at St Cleer
is easily accessible and in good condition. The fine stone build-

ing which covers the well dates from the fifteenth century, though the whole site was restored in 1864.

St Anne's Well/Virtuous Well, Trellech, Gwent

Location: Trellech is 4 miles south of Monmouth, and the well is in a field by a lane just to the south-east of the village. (SO 503051)

St Anne's Well is only one of nine wells said to have been in existence around Trellech, each used for curing a different ailment. St Anne's was also used for making wishes, by dropping a pebble into the water and watching the bubbles which came to the surface. Many bubbles meant that the wish would be granted, a few bubbles meant a delay, no bubbles showed that the wish was in vain.

St Edith's Well, Stoke Edith, Hereford & Worcester

Location: Stoke Edith is 6 miles east of Hereford, and the well is in the bank below the church. (SO 604406)

St Edith's Well, Stoke Edith.

It is said that St Edith prayed for water to flow close by when she was building the church, so that she would not have to walk so far to fetch it. This spring came into being in answer to her prayer, and centuries later the water still flows strongly. In past ages it was believed to have healing properties.

St Cybi's Well, Llangybi.

Ffynnon Gybi/St Cybi's Well, Llangybi, Gwynedd

Location: Llangybi is 5 miles north-east of Pwllheli, and a footpath through the churchyard leads across a field and into a valley, where the well is located. (SH 427413)

This was once an important healing centre, possibly founded by St Cybi himself in the sixth century. The building on the left, which may date back to the twelfth century, houses the main bathing pool; the well itself is hidden away behind it. The building adjoining it was added much later, around 1750, as a cottage for the custodian of the well. The ailments said to be cured here were warts, lameness, blindness, scrofula, scurvy and rheumatism. A sacred eel living in the well would coil itself round the patient's legs if his chances of recovery were good.

163

Cloutie Well, Munlochy.

St Boniface's Well/Cloutie Well, Munlochy, Ross & Cromarty/Highland Region

Location: Munlochy is 5 miles north of Inverness, and the well is half a mile to the north-west, beside the A832. (NH 641537)

This is a famous rag well which has now got out of hand: one recent estimate put the number of rags currently surrounding the well at 50,000!

St Ishow's Well, Partrishow, Powys

Location: Partrishow is tucked away in the Black Mountains, and is reached by country lanes to the north-east of Crickhowell. The well is situated at the bottom of the hill, below the church, where a stream passes beneath the road. If you are facing uphill, the well is a short distance off the road to your right, on the church side of the stream. (SO 278223)

The church and well are closely associated and are of ancient origin. The church is well worth seeing, though the only ancient survival is the eleventh-century font.

164

Holy well at Stevington, Bedfordshire

Location: Stevington is 5 miles north-west of Bedford, and the well is close to the church, reached by following a path to the right of the church gate. (TL 991536)

The water which supplies this well comes from the limestone rock on which the church is built. The well has never been known to freeze or to run dry.

Holy well at Stevington.

St Margaret's Well, Binsey, Oxfordshire

Location: The well is in Binsey churchyard, 2 miles north-west of the centre of Oxford and reached by a lane leading north off the A420 at Osney. (SP 486080)

According to legend, the well was founded by St Frideswide, and miracles were performed here. The water had a reputation for being able to cure eye troubles and to restore fertility in barren women, and it was patronised by the wealthy as well as by the common folk, two famous visitors being King Henry VIII and Katherine of Aragon. Today the well has degenerated into a wishing well.

St Winifred's Well, Woolston, Shropshire

Location: Close to the hamlet of Woolston, which is 4 miles south-east of Oswestry. (SJ 322244)

There may once have been a chapel over this well, but today the visitor sees a tiny half-timbered cottage built directly over the

The water of St Winifred's Well emerges beneath the cottage and flows through the stone troughs just visible below the window.

water, dating back to the sixteenth or seventeenth century and originally used as a court-house. This suggests that Woolston Well was an ancient meeting place or moot, where matters of civil law and local custom were decided. Other places to be so used have included mounds, stones and trees.

Behind and below the cottage are stone troughs through which the water still flows strongly, and which could be dammed to form bathing pools when needed. The water was said to be good for healing wounds, bruises and broken bones.

St Seiriol's Well, Penmon, Anglesey, Gwynedd

Location: Penmon is at the easterly tip of the island, beyond Beaumaris, and the well is below a cliff just behind the priory. (SH 631808)

This well is of ancient origin, dating back at least as far as the sixth century when St Seiriol settled here. Just to the left of the well is a ring of stones which are thought to be the foundations of the cell where he lived. The well-house itself is probably no more than two hundred years old. This is a lovely spot to visit out of the tourist season, with the old priory and the fine dovecot of *c.* 1600; and not far away to the north-west is a cross dating from *c.* 1100.

167

14. *King Arthur: the man and the myth*

King Arthur and his knights lie sleeping beneath the hills, and when Britain's need is greatest they will awake and once more ride forth to vanquish the foe. So runs the old legend with its aura of mystery, pageantry and patriotism. It has become attached to several locations, including Craig-y-Dinas, the Rock of the Fortress, in the Vale of Neath (Mid Glamorgan), Sewingshields Crags (Northumberland), Alderley Edge (Cheshire), and the Eildon Hills (Roxburgh/Borders Region – see 'Places to Visit').

There are over 150 places in Britain with supposed Arthurian connections, places where events in Arthur's life are supposed to have happened. But the truth is, we cannot even be sure that King Arthur ever existed! The familiar legend tells how he was born at Tintagel Castle, the son of Ygraine and Uther Pendragon, King of England (who entered Ygraine's bed disguised as her husband). The infant Arthur was claimed by Merlin the magician and raised by a knight, until at the age of fifteen he was proclaimed king after having successfully pulled a sword from the stone in which it was embedded. This sword was later broken in battle and Arthur was taken by Merlin to a lake where the Lady of the Lake gave him a magic sword called Excalibur.

Arthur and his knights would meet round the magnificent round table he received as a present at his marriage to Guinevere, and there they would plan their adventures and exploits, the best-known of them being the Quest for the Holy Grail. But Arthur also had domestic problems. Guinevere had fallen in love with Lancelot, a knight who had been raised by the Lady of the Lake. When Arthur learned of this, Lancelot and Guinevere fled to France, with Arthur and his army in pursuit. But in his absence, trouble was brewing in England. Arthur's son Mordred, a child born of unwitting incest between Arthur and Morgause his half-sister, had seized Arthur's crown, and on Arthur's return the two forces met in a mighty battle at Camlann. Arthur killed Mordred, but Mordred had struck Arthur

The site of King Arthur's tomb in Glastonbury Abbey, but as the notice makes clear, not the site where the bodies were originally found. (See the entry for Glastonbury Abbey in 'Places to Visit'.)

SITE OF KING ARTHUR'S TOMB.
IN THE YEAR 1101 THE BODIES OF
KING ARTHUR AND HIS QUEEN WERE
SAID TO HAVE BEEN FOUND ON THE
SOUTH SIDE OF THE LADY CHAPEL.
ON 19TH APRIL 1278 THEIR REMAINS WERE
REMOVED IN THE PRESENCE OF
KING EDWARD I AND QUEEN ELEANOR
TO A BLACK MARBLE TOMB ON THIS SITE.
THIS TOMB SURVIVED UNTIL THE
DISSOLUTION OF THE ABBEY IN 1539

with his sword, and the blow proved fatal. Before he died, Arthur told his knight Bedivere to throw Excalibur back into the lake, and on doing this a hand reached up to grasp it by the hilt and draw it beneath the surface. Arthur, still alive, was taken by barge to Avalon, where he died.

Scholars have tried to trace all the strands of the Arthurian story, including side-plots not mentioned in the brief summary above, back to their origins, and have found that they stem from a number of sources, including the *Historia Regum Britanniae* (History of the Kings of Britain) by Geoffrey of Monmouth, which its author claimed was true history, but which is now known to be a collection of legends, traditions, and assorted rumours, much of it of dubious veracity. This dates from about 1136, over six hundred years after King Arthur's supposed death, and therefore is unlikely to have been very factually accurate anyway. Later in the same century several French poets wrote romances elaborating the 'facts' about Arthur, and then in the mid fifteenth century came Sir Thomas Malory's *Morte d'Arthur*, followed by even more recent poems by Tennyson and others. One thing we can feel sure of is that today's legends bear little resemblance to historical fact, whatever that may be!

Some historians think that Arthur may have been a real person, a warrior chieftain who lived in the Dark Ages, the time immediately after the Romans abandoned Britain. The decisive battle of Badon about 500 was won by someone called Arthur, who led the Britons and defeated the Saxons led by Hengist. The location of this battle is not known. It was probably in the south of England, possibly at one of the several Badburys, or even in the Bath area. However it is possible that the site of Arthur's headquarters, known as Camelot, has been located. Although there are other contenders, Camelot has been associated with South Cadbury Castle in Somerset since 1542 when the antiquary John Leland wrote: 'At the very south end of the church of South-Cadbyri standeth Camallate, sometime a famous town or castle ... The people can tell nothing there but that they have heard say Arthur much resorted to Camalat.' This supposed association was greatly strengthened in the late 1960s when a large-scale excavation was carried out at South Cadbury Castle by Leslie Alcock, who discovered that the Iron Age hillfort had been reoccupied and refortified by someone of importance, and at just the time when Arthur would have been active.

If South Cadbury Castle gives us hope, a site which might at first glance seem to provide conclusive proof of Arthur's existence has several question-marks attached to it. This is the site of Arthur's grave at Glastonbury Abbey (Somerset). This was accidentally found by monks in 1190 or 1191. At a depth of 7 feet they discovered a stone slab and a lead cross, the latter with a Latin inscription:. HIC IACET SEPULTUS INCLITUS REX ARTURIUS IN INSULA AVALONIA. 'Here lies buried the renowned King Arthur in the Isle of Avalon.' Nine feet below that was a hollowed log, Arthur's coffin. The bones of two people were found, a tall man with his skull damaged as if by a blow, and smaller bones together with a scrap of yellow hair. Although this event has long been thought to be a hoax perpetrated by the monks as a fund-raising venture, the fact is that in 1962 Dr Ralegh Radford excavated the site and confirmed that the monks had dug there, and had found an early grave. But was it really the grave of Arthur and Guinevere? The inscribed cross has unfortunately been lost, but a drawing dating from 1607 survives and scholars say that the lettering is not twelfth-century work. However, although they agree that it is earlier than twelfth century, they cannot agree on a date, so the question as to the grave's authenticity must remain unanswered, at least for the present.

Over the centuries, the Arthurian romance has taken a hold on the national consciousness and, factual or not, become part of our history. Each area wanted to lay claim to Arthurian connections, and many landscape features thus acquired names linking them with the Arthurian legend, or were pointed out as places where Arthur had fought a great battle. The legendary King Arthur grew to gigantic proportions in the eyes of the rural population – hence Arthur's Chair, a Devon rock formation; Arthur's Seat, a hill east of Edinburgh; Arthur's Bed, a coffin-shaped piece of granite on Bodmin Moor; Arthur's Quoit, nine of these in Wales; Arthur's Table or Round Table, several earthworks given this name, including the amphitheatre at Caerleon (see Chapter 10); and many others.

The exploits of King Arthur, his knights, and his relatives, were in folklore located at diverse places – for example the battle of Camlann, at which he was fatally wounded, was claimed for Slaughter Bridge near Camelford (Cornwall), where a memorial slab is called Arthur's Tomb; or Camlann was on Salisbury Plain (Wiltshire) or on Snowdon (Gwynedd) or by the River Cam (Somerset), and so on. Other examples of legendary Arthurian locations will be found in 'Places to Visit', but anyone wishing to explore further the intricate links between the legend of King Arthur and the British landscape is recommended to read Geoffrey Ashe's *A Guidebook to Arthurian Britain*, an exhaustive exploration of Arthurian lore.

PLACES TO VISIT

Tintagel Castle, Cornwall

Location: Tintagel is on the north coast, 12 miles north of Bodmin, and the castle is a short walk from the village. (SX 049891)

This dramatic headland, with its steep and rock-strewn shores, is the ideal location for the birth of our national hero. But it is impossible to prove conclusively that he was born here. The remains of buildings have been excavated, but they cannot be precisely dated or their function ascertained. There may have been a fifth- or sixth-century monastery at Tintagel, or possibly

Tintagel Castle.

a fifth-century chieftain's dwelling – and if it was the latter, then it is not impossible that Arthur could have begun life here. Geoffrey of Monmouth in his *History* chose to locate Arthur's birth at Tintagel, when he would have been expected to choose Wales as the more likely location, since many strands of the Arthurian story originated in Wales and Geoffrey himself was a Welshman.

Regardless of the Arthurian connections, Tintagel Castle is worth visiting for its site alone. Try to go there on a stormy day, out of season, for it swarms with tourists in the summer. The large cave you will see at the foot of the cliff is known as Merlin's Cave and is said to be haunted by his ghost.

South Cadbury Castle, Somerset

Location: The village of South Cadbury is 5 miles north of Sherborne, and the hillfort is reached along a track just south of the church. (ST 628252)

The banks and ditches of the Iron Age hillfort are still very prominent all around the hilltop, from where on a clear day the views are marvellous. The refortification of the hilltop during Arthur's time was done on a massive scale, and it was clearly an important stronghold – possibly Arthur's Camelot. Unfortunately there is nothing left to see of the fifth-century buildings, which were constructed largely of timber. Stone ramparts were uncovered during the excavations, and the foundations of a timber hall 63 feet by 34 feet were found on the high part of the hill. Traces of a timber gatehouse guarding the south-west approach to the hilltop were found, and evidence that the hilltop had been strongly defended with timber walls on top of the stone ramparts. The whole of the hilltop was not excavated, only sections, and the outlines of other buildings probably await discovery; perhaps there will also be conclusive proof that this was indeed Camelot.

Dozmary Pool, Cornwall

Location: On Bodmin Moor, north-east of Bodmin and reached along a lane off the A30 at Jamaica Inn. (SX 195745)

This is one of several stretches of water where the knight Sir Bedivere is said to have thrown Arthur's sword Excalibur back to its owner. As it is nowhere near any of the places where the

Dozmary Pool.

battle of Camlann may have been fought, the identification is unlikely to be correct. Other waters suggested include Loe or Looe Pool which is an inlet of Mount's Bay (Cornwall) now divided from the sea by a sandy ridge; a lake at Bosherston (Dyfed), Llyn Llydaw below Snowdon (Gwynedd), and, perhaps the most likely location, Glastonbury, where the sword was thrown from Pomparles Bridge. For us, though, Dozmary Pool has a suitably desolate and lonely feeling, and it is not too difficult to imagine Sir Bedivere's doubts and hesitations before the deed was finally accomplished.

Glastonbury Tor, Somerset

Location: Glastonbury is 11 miles east of Bridgwater, and the Tor is just to the east of the town, reached along narrow lanes. (ST 512386)

Glastonbury has long been known as the island of Avalon, and maybe it was. It was certainly once an island: before the relatively recent drainage schemes the whole of the surrounding area was swampland and often flooded. Traces of Celtic lake-

Glastonbury Tor.

174

villages have been found nearby. The Tor itself is a landmark visible from miles around, a strange conical hill seeming to offer entry to another world. Its slopes are ridged, and some people have been able to trace a spiral path along the ridges, winding round and round the hill to the summit, possibly a route taken by pilgrims making a long and arduous ascent of the sacred hill. In legend the Tor can give access to the fairy land of Annwn, and the sixth-century saint Collen is said to have paid a brief visit to the fairy palace, when invited by the king of the fairies, Gwyn ap Nudd. He entered the palace and was offered food by the king, but knowing this to be a trap, St Collen spilled the holy water he had secretly brought with him, and immediately the king, his courtiers and palace disappeared and St Collen found himself alone on the silent Tor.

A church dedicated to St Michael was built on the summit by monks, but this was later demolished by an earthquake. The tower standing there now is all that remains of a later church, also dedicated to St Michael. The hill's supposed Arthurian connection comes from Caradoc's *Life of Gildas*. According to this, Arthur's wife Guinevere was kidnapped by Melwas, king of Somerset, and taken to his stronghold which was probably on the Tor. Excavations in the 1960s did find traces of buildings of Arthurian date. Arthur arrived with an army to rescue his wife, but a treaty was arranged in time to prevent a battle.

Chalice Well, Glastonbury, Somerset

Location: In a garden at the foot of the Tor, maintained by the Chalice Well Trust and open to the public. (ST 507385)

The high iron content of this spring water gives a reddish colouring which has given rise to the belief that the water contains blood, hence the well's other name, Blood Spring. It has also initiated the legend that hidden within the deeper recesses of the well is the Chalice of the Holy Grail containing the blood of Christ, which colours the water. The spring probably supplied water to a small religious community below the Tor many centuries ago; it also seems to be mentioned in *The High History of the Holy Grail*, so its Grail connections are not totally spurious. The spring itself is kept covered, with a lid designed by Frederick Bligh Bond who carried out excavations at the abbey, but the water can be tasted at an outlet in the lower part of the garden.

176

Chalice Well, Glastonbury.

Glastonbury Abbey, Somerset

Location: In the town centre, approached through an archway
by the Town Wall. (ST 500388)

The ruins to be seen today date from the late twelfth century
and even in their ruinous condition the towering walls give
some indication of the former glory of this abbey, one of the
largest and wealthiest in Britain until the Dissolution in the
sixteenth century. The abbey was preceded by a monastery,
which was destroyed by fire in 1184. One of the older buildings
was a church dedicated to the Virgin Mary and said to have been
built by Joseph of Arimathea who according to legend brought
the Holy Grail to England and settled at Glastonbury. The
Holy Thorn which flowers at Christmas grew from his staff,
and offspring from the parent tree can still be seen in the abbey
grounds and in front of St John's church. On the site of St

177

Mary's church now stands the ruin of the later Lady Chapel, illustrated here.

The Lady Chapel at Glastonbury Abbey, beside which was the monastery burial-ground where the monks claimed to have found the grave of King Arthur. The bones were later placed in a black marble tomb in front of the high altar, which is the site today marked as the 'Site of King Arthur's tomb' (illustrated earlier in this chapter).

The Tristan Stone, Cornwall

Location: Beside the A3082, just west of Fowey. (SX 112522)

This stone is not in its original position and may also have been broken, but despite the vicissitudes of its past, the worn inscription has survived long enough to be read as: DRUSTANUS HIC IACIT CUNOMORI FILIUS – 'Drustanus lies here, son of Cunomorus'. Drustanus is an alternative form of Tristan, and he is thought to have been the same as the Tristan who was one of King Arthur's knights. The monument dates from the sixth century and therefore belongs to the right period. Tristan fell in love with Iseult, the young wife of King Mark, who was Tristan's father. Not far away is Castle Dore, an earthwork which was first occupied in the Iron Age, and then reoccupied from the fifth to seventh centuries. There are various clues which suggest that it was the court of Cynvawr or Cunomorus, ruler of

178

Dumnonia (which included Cornwall), and the same Cunomorus as is named on the Tristan Stone. In order to tie up the loose ends of the story, it has been suggested that Cunomorus and Mark were the same person, but no firm conclusion can be drawn about this.

Castell Dinas Bran, Clwyd

Location: Just outside the town of Llangollen. (SJ 222431)

This prominent hill was fortified in the Iron Age, and earth banks can still be traced. In medieval times a castle was built, whose ruins still crown the hilltop. The Bran of the name was a legendary British hero, whose head acted as a protection against the might of the Saxons, so long as it remained buried in Tower Hill in London. King Arthur dug it up, believing that the people should rely on the army, not on magical charms. In a thirteenth-century French romance on the Quest for the Holy Grail, the Grail is said to be hidden in a castle named as 'Chastiel Bran'. The story is set in the Welsh Marches, and there is talk of fishing in the river, so some people believe that Castell Dinas Bran, with the River Dee flowing close by, was intended. Another name for the Grail Castle was Corbin, which is an old French word meaning crow or raven; 'Bran' also means raven. It seems therefore that at one time this imposing citadel, which dominates the Dee valley hereabouts, was identified as the place where the Holy Grail lies hidden.

Castell Dinas Bran.

Maen Hueil, Ruthin, Clwyd

Location: Ruthin is 13 miles north-west of Wrexham, and the stone is beside Barclay's Bank in St Peter's Square. (SJ 123583)

Hueil was one of Arthur's adversaries in Wales, according to legend. They fought a duel over one of Arthur's mistresses and Arthur's knee was wounded as a result, but he said that peace would be maintained between them if Hueil kept quiet about the wound. Later, Arthur visited Ruthin disguised as a woman, to visit another lady friend, and while he was at a dance Hueil saw him and recognised him. He made a comment about Arthur's lameness, and as a result Arthur had him arrested and then beheaded him on this stone in the market place. Although this story is almost certainly total fantasy, Hueil may have been a local chieftain living in the hills nearby.

Eildon Hills, Roxburgh/Borders Region

Location: A mile south of Melrose. (NT 5432)

This is one of several places in Britain where Arthur and his knights are supposed to lie sleeping in a cave, awaiting the call

Eildon Hills.

to come to Britain's aid. A story tells how a horse-dealer called Canonbie Dick was taken to see the sleeping men by a stranger who had offered to buy two horses from him. Inside the cave he saw Arthur and his knights asleep, with their horses, and a table on which were a sword and a horn. Given the choice between drawing the sword or sounding the horn, he chose the latter but was told that he had made the wrong choice, and had not acquitted himself as a warrior should. He lost the chance to join King Arthur's men and a strong wind swept him from the cave. Afterwards when he told some shepherds his story he immediately dropped dead; no one could ever locate the entrance to the cave.

15. *Dragonlore*

The concept of the dragon as a bringer of fertility may not be a familiar one, but carvings of dragons with foliage sprouting from their tails and bunches of grapes or fruits issuing from their mouths can be seen in many churches around the country (see for example Llananno in 'Places to Visit'). In the Far East the dragon represented beneficence and supernatural wisdom, while in the Christian tradition he embodied the power of evil, or the Devil. Originally the dragon had strong fertility connections and in all likelihood it was this aspect which was predominant in pre-Christian times. The church carvings may, like the green men we described in Chapter 11, be a sign of the continuation of pagan beliefs within the Christian tradition, or conversely a means of averting what the Christian hierarchy saw as pagan evil by using its own symbols against it. In churches the dragon is more often seen in his death-throes, being slain by a saint like St George or St Michael, and there he quite clearly symbolises the evil powers of darkness being ousted by Christian virtue.

This theme of dragon-slaying spread out from the Christian Church into the rural communities, with the result that in many areas there were strong traditions of local dragons being outwitted and killed by local heroes, using a variety of ingenious methods. At Llanrhaeadr-ym-Mochnant (Clwyd), the people covered a standing stone with red cloth and hidden spikes. The dragon, in this case a flying specimen, inflamed by the colour red, battered himself to death against the stone. Since this event the stone has been known as Post Coch (Red Pillar) or Post-y-Wiber (Pillar of the Viper) and can still be seen, in a field just outside the village. A wyvern (two-legged dragon) was also vulnerable to the colour red at Newcastle Emlyn (Dyfed). He lived in the castle and was a fire-breathing nuisance, so the soldier detailed to shoot him first threw a piece of red cloth into the river. While the wyvern was distractedly attacking the cloth, the soldier shot him through the navel, the only vulner-

This dramatic bench-end carving in Withersfield church (Suffolk) depicts a dragon being despatched by a brave knight, possibly intended to be St George himself. The horse looks distinctly apprehensive about the whole affair, but despite his puny sword the knight is clearly in control and the dragon lies on his back in an attitude of surrender.

182

able place in the creature's tough hide. As Jacqueline Simpson remarks in her study *British Dragons*, it is remarkable that a reptile should possess a navel, and perhaps the vent was intended, that and the mouth being the only two vulnerable places in such a creature.

The farmer who killed the worm of Cnoc-na-Cnoimh (Worm's Hill, 'worm' being another name for the dragon) in Sutherland (Highland Region) did so with the aid of a burning peat dipped in boiling pitch and stuck on the end of a long spear. The fumes were suffocating to the dragon, which wound itself tightly around the hill, until the farmer approached near enough to quickly thrust the peat down his throat and thus kill him.

One of the best known of British dragons was the Lambton Worm (Durham) who began life as an ugly worm caught on the end of a fishing line in the River Wear by the heir to Lambton Castle. He threw it into a well (later known as Worm Well) where it grew fast and soon emerged to spend the day coiled round a rock in the middle of the river. At night it moved to a neighbouring hill (Worm Hill near Fatfield) around which it could coil its long body three times. It preyed on lambs and cows' milk and having devastated the countryside round about, it moved across the river to the estate of Lambton Castle. A large trough filled with the milk of nine cows was provided for it every morning, and it caused havoc if the quantity was reduced. During all this time, the young heir was away from the castle, fighting in distant wars. Although many gallant knights had come to slay the dragon, none was successful, its severed limbs immediately reuniting with the body. In due course the young heir returned and determined to solve the problem, having been told by a wise woman that it was he himself who had been the cause of all the trouble. He had a suit of armour made which was studded with spear blades and then, holding his sword, he stood on a rock in mid-stream, having first vowed that if he was successful, he would kill the first living creature he met afterwards, or else the Lords of Lambton would for nine generations never die in their beds. When the dragon came, he stood firm and struck out at it. Enraged, it coiled itself around him and cut itself badly on the blades, so that the river ran red with blood. The blood loss weakened it, and as soon as its embrace lessened, the knight drew his sword and cut it in two. One part was carried off in the river, and being unable to reunite, the dragon died. The knight blew his horn to alert the household, and to warn them to release his favourite hound, which was to be the sacrifice of the first living creature he met. But the old Lord was so excited he rushed forward himself. The knight could not kill his father and again blew his horn, upon which the dog ran forward and the knight slew him. But in vain, for he had broken his vow, and thenceforth the family was cursed.

The story of the Lambton Worm is typical of many of the British dragon stories, even though the method of dispatching the monster varies. Many other examples can be found in the two fine books on dragons written by Jacqueline Simpson and Ralph Whitlock (see Bibliography), and some are also included in our 'Places to Visit'. Are these stories simply folktales, or do they have a deeper or symbolic significance? In our earlier book *The Secret Country* we noted the number of prehistoric sites with dragon legends attached to them, and the number of legends telling of hoards of treasure watched over by dragons, and we wondered whether in such cases the dragon was a symbol of the earth energy which prehistoric men might have utilised – an energy which, if carelessly handled, could cause havoc and destruction just as the dragons do in the traditional tales.

Another possibility is that dragons were real creatures. A pamphlet was published in 1614, titled 'A True and Wonderful Discourse relating a strange and monstrous Serpent (or Dragon) lately discovered, and yet living, to the great Annoyance and divers Slaughters of both Men and Cattell, by his strong and violent Poison: in Sussex, two Miles from Horsam, in a Woode called St Leonard's Forrest, and thirtie Miles from London, this present Month of August, 1614. With the true Generation of Serpents.' In this pamphlet the creature is described as

> nine feete, or rather more, in length, and shaped almost in the forme of an axle-tree of a cart; a quantitie of thickness in the middest, and somewhat smaller at both endes. The former part, which he shootes forth as a necke, is supposed to be an elle long; with a white ring, as it were, of scales about it. The scales along his backe seem to be blackish, and so much as is discovered under his bellie, appeareth to be red; ... It is likewise discovered to have large feete, but the eye may be there deceived; for some suppose that serpents have no feete ... [He] rids away (as we call it) as fast as a man can run. He is of countenance very proud, and at the sight or hearing of men or cattel, will raise his neck upright, and seem to listen and looke about, with great arrogancy. There are likewise upon either side of him discovered, two great bunches so big as a large foote-ball, and (as some thinke) will in time grow to wings, but God, I hope, will (to defend the poor people in the neighbourhood) that he shall be destroyed before he grow so fledge.

The dragon was thought to live on rabbits; although he (or rather the 'venome' he shot forth) killed dogs and people, he did not eat them. It is also interesting that always 'in his track or path [he] left a glutinous and slimie matter ... which is very corrupt and offensive to the scent ...' No one has yet been able to suggest a known animal which fits the description of the St Leonard's Forest 'dragon'. Was it a water monster living temporarily on land? There have been reports that the Loch Ness Monster has been seen on land, and also reports of Irish lake monsters moving from one small lough to another. Perhaps the St Leonard's Forest monster and the present-day lake monsters (see Chapter 20 for more details) belong to the same species, and perhaps there were once more of them around, living in lakes and rivers and other wet places and occasionally venturing out to vary their diet with cattle and sheep. Perhaps they have today retreated to the more remote lakes of Scotland and Ireland because in past centuries the bold knights were so successful in slaughtering them!

PLACES TO VISIT

Llananno church, Powys

Location: 10 miles south of Newtown, and 1 mile north-west of Llanbister, between the River Ithon and the A483. (SO 096743)

The old church of St Anno was rebuilt a hundred years ago, but the marvellous screen of the fifteenth–sixteenth century was retained. Among the fine carving can be found wyverns or dragons with vines sprouting from their mouths, a symbol of the continuing preoccupation with the theme of fertility, with which Man should always be vitally concerned, whatever his religious persuasion, for without fertility we die.

Linton church, Roxburgh/Borders Region

Location: 8 miles north-east of Jedburgh. (NT 773262)

The Linton Worm's haunt was Wormistone or Linton Hill, which still bears the marks made when he coiled his body tightly round it. The knight who slew him was John Somerville, and he used almost the same method as described earlier

Linton church.

when we wrote of the Worm of Cnoc-na-Cnoimh. A peat was
fastened to a wheel on the end of a spear and dipped in boiling
resin, brimstone and pitch before being thrust down the hapless
beast's throat. This event is commemorated on a tympanum
above the church door, but sadly the carving is now very worn
and the detail is hard to discern. The hill where it all happened
can be seen from the churchyard. John Somerville was knight-
ed in the late twelfth century, and created first Baron of
Linton. The family used a dragon as their crest, and the more
prosaic historians try to tell us that the dragon crest and the
picture on the worn carving came first, the dragon-slaying tale
being an invention woven around them.

187

Wissington church, Suffolk

Location: Just north of the River Stour which forms the Suffolk/Essex border; 1 mile south-west of Nayland. (TL 955332)

In this Norman church to which the Victorians added a number of pseudo-Norman features has survived a series of fine wall-paintings dating from the thirteenth century, showing, among other subjects, the Wise Men in bed being warned in a dream not to return to Herod, St Francis preaching to the birds, the Nativity, the Adoration of the Magi, and a fine dragon. Another church with a dragon wall-painting is at Ford (West Sussex).

Uffington church, Oxfordshire

Location: 9 miles east of Swindon. (SU 302893)

We have already described and illustrated (see Chapter 12) the great white horse or dragon cut out of the chalk on White Horse Hill, and Dragon Hill below it, where, according to legend, St George killed the dragon, a bare white patch remaining to show where its blood was spilt. Not far away in Uffington church the dragon motif continues. The thirteenth-century church has an imposing appearance with its attractive octagonal tower. Until the eighteenth century this tower was surmounted by a spire, but it fell during a storm. The south doorway has carved serpent heads, and until earlier in this century there were two eighteenth-century brass candelabra inside the church which each held twelve candles in a serpent's mouth with a dove hovering above. Now a modern dragon-carving adorns the font cover.

Low Ham church, Somerset

Location: 1 mile east-north-east of Langport. (ST 432291)

This imitation Gothic seventeenth-century church stands alone in a field; the earthworks close by are the remains of a mansion which was never completed. Inside can be seen the spear shown in the photograph. This is said to be the spear used by John Aller to kill the flying serpent which was terrorising the area around Aller to the west. It poisoned crops and trees by its very presence, and like the Lambton Worm it was very fond of milk.

John Aller determined to overcome the monster, and so he first of all covered himself with pitch and put on a mask to protect himself against the dragon's poisonous breath. He took his spear, which had been specially made for the purpose, and attacked the dragon at night while it slept in its den. He killed it and then had the entrance to the den blocked with an iron harrow to prevent the baby dragons inside from escaping.

Low Ham spear.

Brent Pelham church, Hertfordshire

Location: 7 miles north-west of Bishop's Stortford.
(TL 433308)

Inside the church the tomb of the dragon-slayer Piers Shonks can be seen. He was Lord of the Manor and the earthworks at the site of his moated house can still be seen to the east of the village. Some time during the thirteenth century Piers Shonks slew the fiercesome dragon which lived in a cave beneath an ancient yew tree. He killed it by thrusting his spear down its throat, but this act greatly enraged the Devil, whose favourite the dragon was. He vowed to have Shonks' body and soul when he died, whether he was buried inside or outside the church. Shonks said that he would choose where he lay after death, and when he was dying he shot an arrow at the church to locate his burial place. The arrow struck the north wall of the nave, and the tomb was placed inside the wall – out of reach of the Devil, for it is neither inside nor outside the church. Another hero, Jack o' Kent, cheated the Devil in a similar way, by ensuring that he was buried in the thickness of the wall at Grosmont church (Gwent).

The carvings on Piers Shonks' tomb show an angel carrying a soul away (which may have initiated the story of the Devil taking Shonks' soul) and a dragon with a cross in its mouth (which may have initiated the story of the dragon killed by a spear thrust into its mouth). A verse above the tomb is thought to have been added in the seventeenth century by the vicar of the time. It is in Latin and English, the English part reading:

> O PIERS SHONKS
> WHO DIED ANNO 1086
>
> Nothing of Cadmus or St George, those names
> Of great renown, survives them but their fames;
> Time was so sharp set as to make no Bones
> Of theirs, nor of their monumental Stones.
> But Shonks one serpent kills, t'other defies,
> And in this wall, as in a fortress, lies.

Crowcombe church, Somerset

Location: In the Quantock Hills, 9 miles north-west of Taunton. (ST 141367)

We have already illustrated one of the fine sixteenth-century bench-end carvings in this church (see Chapter 11), and we

190

Crowcombe bench-end.

cannot omit the bench-end which shows a dragon-slaying, perhaps the finest carving of this kind in Britain, certainly the finest we have yet seen. Two men are dealing with a ferocious two-headed dragon, and using a method similar to some we have already described – pushing a burning peat down its throat. The bottom half of the panel is taken up with fruiting vines, a clear reference to the dragon's fertility aspect, since the vines are emerging from the mouth of another dragon tucked away in the bottom lefthand corner. So this panel combines the two opposing aspects of the dragon – the evil and the beneficent. A local legend has grown up around this bench-end, telling that it depicts the slaying of a monster by a man from Crowcombe. In fact Somerset is particularly rich in dragon legends. Apart from Crowcombe there are such legends at Aller (see Low Ham elsewhere in 'Places to Visit'), Carhampton, Castle Neroche, Churchstanton, Kilve, Kingston St Mary, Norton Fitzwarren and Shervage Wood.

Llyn Cynwch, Gwynedd

Location: 2 miles north of Dolgellau, approached from the north-east, along the route of the Precipice Walk. (SH 7320)

Llyn Cynwch.

A forerunner of the Loch Ness Monster was said to dwell in this

lake, a wyvern known as Gwiber Coed y Moch which would crawl out of the water and up into the mountains. Any living creature caught by the Gwiber's eye became helpless. Eventually it was killed by a shepherd who cut off its head with an axe when he came across it asleep. A cairn of stones piled over the body is still known as Carnedd y Wiber (Serpent's Cairn).

16. *Mazes: the ritual dance*

The earliest known mazes or labyrinths may be around 3,000 years old. They are rock carvings in the Camonica Valley in the Italian Alps, and although they cannot be dated precisely, some of the carvings are believed to be prehistoric, with others added at later dates. The origins of the maze symbol are difficult to trace, and there may well be earlier examples not yet discovered. Some of the carvings we illustrated in Chapter 6, for example the cup and ring marks, and the triple spiral and entrance stone at Newgrange, have strong similarities to maze designs, and there are many other examples of Neolithic rock art which are also labyrinthine in concept. There may also have been labyrinthine buildings in ancient Egypt and in other early civilisations, notably at Knossos on Crete.

In legend the Cretan labyrinth is linked with the story of Theseus and the Minotaur. The labyrinth was built by Daedalus on the instructions of Minos, King of Crete (who later became a judge in Hades, the underworld – one of the numerous links to be found between the labyrinth and death). The labyrinth housed the Minotaur, half bull, half man, who was the offspring of Minos's wife, Pasiphaë, and a bull. The Athenians, as a result of some past adventure, were bound to send Minos seven young boys and seven maidens every ninth year (different authorities give different periods), and these were offered to the Minotaur. Theseus, the great Athenian hero, may have been among the tribute on one occasion. Be that as it may, he resolved to kill the Minotaur, for if that could be done the tribute would thereafter be cancelled. Minos's daughter Ariadne was attracted by Theseus, and wishing to help him she took the advice of Daedalus and gave him a clue of thread by which he could retrace his steps and escape from the labyrinth. Reaching the centre, he killed the Minotaur and leaving the labyrinth with the boys and girls intended for sacrifice, they all set sail for home. En route, they landed on Delos, where they celebrated their victory with the Crane Dance.

J. G. Frazer's interpretation of the Minotaur story, given in *The Golden Bough*, is an interesting one. He concludes:

> On the whole the foregoing evidence ... points to the conclusion that at Cnossus the king represented the sun-god, and that every eight years his divine powers were renewed at a great festival, which comprised, first, the sacrifice of human victims by fire to a bull-headed image of the sun, and second, the marriage of the king disguised as a bull to the queen disguised as a cow, the two personating respectively the sun and the moon.

The symbol of the labyrinth was also used elsewhere. An Etruscan terracotta wine-jar from Tragliatella, Italy, dating from the late seventh century BC and probably predating the Cretan Knossos, shows a maze and people in procession, possibly depicting funeral rites. The maze may have been used to keep evil influences from the grave, and at the same time to show the initiate the route of death and rebirth. The recurring links with death again remind us of the maze-like spiral designs carved on the walls of a number of Neolithic tombs in Britain and Ireland.

During the several hundred years BC the maze symbol spread far and wide. Elaborate mazes have been found on Roman

Mazes of stones are found mainly in Scandinavia, but there are also examples in the Scilly Isles, this one being on St Agnes. It was said to have been made in 1726 by a lighthouse keeper, but he was probably renewing an earlier maze. Known as Troy Town, it was photographed in 1885 along with the wreck of the Earl of Lonsdale.

mosaic pavements, two British examples being at Caerleon (Gwent) where a damaged mosaic was discovered in 1866 in the churchyard, and at Harpham (Humberside) where a large pavement was discovered in 1904 during the excavation of a Roman villa. It is now on display on a wall by the staircase in the City Hall, Kingston-upon-Hull. The maze was also adopted by the early Christians, symbolising for them the path of life, and the design was carved on walls or made into pavements in churches and cathedrals, especially in Italy and France, with some painted mazes in Scandinavian churches. There are a few church mazes in Britain, the earliest possibly being the simple maze carved on the Norman font in Lewannick church (Cornwall). A fifteenth-century roof boss in St Mary Redcliffe church, Bristol (Avon) has a maze carving only 4 inches across. Thornton church (Leicestershire) has a simple spiral maze of large stones, probably of pre-Reformation date, and the only two pavement mazes in British churches are at Bourn and Ely Cathedral (both in Cambridgeshire). Alkborough church (Humberside) also has two mazes (see 'Places to Visit').

A typical unicursal maze, this one being the turf maze formerly on Ripon Common (North Yorkshire).

There are many types of designs used for mazes over the centuries, and the origins of any particular example can often be ascertained from the design used. The differences between the designs are too complex to describe here, but they can be found in books on this subject (see Bibliography). The main feature of the ancient maze designs, of course, is that there is only one path from the entrance to the centre, with no side-tracks (a unicursal maze). The turf mazes which were once widespread in Britain are of this kind, and they are thought to have derived from church designs. The earliest may date from medieval times. The number of ancient turf mazes now surviving is very small. Many have been destroyed by cultivation or building, and many more have been lost through neglect – the grass must be cut regularly else they are quickly overgrown. The mazes which can still be seen are at Alkborough (Humberside), Wing (Leicestershire), Hilton (Cambridgeshire), Brandsby (North Yorkshire), Breamore (Hampshire), St Catherine's Hill, Winchester (Hampshire), Saffron Walden (Essex) and Somerton (Oxfordshire), several of these being described and illustrated in 'Places to Visit'.

The name given to one now-lost maze, The Shepherd's Race at Boughton Green (Northamptonshire) and the fact that the treading of its path was a popular event in the annual three-day fair, indicates that running the maze was often part of local festivities, a link back many centuries to the days when funeral

This beautifully maintained turf maze is in a private garden at Somerton (Oxfordshire). Known as Troy Town, its path is 400 yards in length.

197

rituals and other dances were performed at mazes. Other names often used for English turf mazes (they were not found in Wales, Scotland or Ireland) hark back to their ancient and foreign origins – Troy Town, Walls of Troy, City of Troy, Miz-Maze, Julian's Bower.

The dances performed at mazes may once have been more elaborate than simply following the path of the maze. Some of the traditional dances still performed in Britain may have originated as maze dances. One such is the Abbot's Bromley Horn Dance (Staffordshire – see Chapter 18). Here the dancers carry sets of reindeer antlers with carved wooden reindeer heads fixed to them, three sets painted white, three black, and holding these before them, they perform a dance in single file. Every so often the leader doubles back, after having led the others into a circle; the blacks and whites are then face to face and engage in symbolic combat, after which the procession begins again.

The meaning of this ritual dance is unknown, though it has been suggested that it may be a relic of a hunting dance. Its symbolism probably goes far deeper, and it has also been suggested that the 'battle' signifies the struggle between life and death, the white symbolising life and the black death. The single-file twisting dance has echoes of a maze dance; and the antlers and animal heads may possibly symbolise the Minotaur. The Crane Dance of Delos, first performed by Theseus and the rescued sacrificial victims, also followed a spiral path, first into the centre to symbolise death, and then out again in the opposite direction, symbolising evolution and rebirth. Other spiral dances were once performed in Britain. In *Cornish Feasts and Folk-lore* by M. A. Courtney (1890) are descriptions of two spiral dances, the 'snails' creep' being described thus:

> The young people being all assembled in a large meadow, the village band strikes up a simple but lively air, and marches forward, followed by the whole assemblage, leading hand-in-hand (or more closely linked in case of engaged couples), the whole keeping time to the tune with a lively step. The band or head of the serpent keeps marching in an ever-narrowing circle, whilst its train of dancing followers becomes coiled around it in circle after circle. It is now that the most interesting part of the dance commences, for the band, taking a sharp turn about, begins to retrace the circle, still followed as before, and a number of young men with long, leafy branches in their hands as standards, direct this counter-movement with almost military precision.

J. G. Frazer associates the Cretan maze with sun-worship, suggesting that the Crane Dance may have been imitating the sun's course, and thus, 'by means of sympathetic magic, to aid the great luminary to run his race on high'. This reminds us of prehistoric man's preoccupation with the movements of the sun and other heavenly bodies, and also the associated fertility aspects. The Morris dancers to be seen so often dancing in country villages and towns in the summer-time (see Chapter 18) are also performing age-old rituals whose origins may lie in prehistoric fertility dances.

The mazes which are probably best known today are the hedge mazes, which have one correct path to the centre but many false routes which when followed become dead-ends (multicursal mazes), hence the popularity of these mazes with youngsters. Hedge mazes became popular in Britain in the sixteenth century. One of the earliest in England was planted at Theobalds (Hertfordshire) *c.* 1560, but was destroyed by Parliamentary troops in the 1640s. The oldest surviving hedge maze in England is at Hampton Court Palace (Greater London), having been planted in 1690 and possibly replacing an even older maze. It is not a complex maze to follow, but its path nevertheless extends for about half a mile. In recent years hedge mazes have again become fashionable and new ones have been planted. In 1978 the world's largest hedge maze, with yew hedges and covering an area of 380 feet by 175 feet, was planted at Longleat House (Wiltshire). The upsurge of interest in mazes shows that even now, in the late twentieth century, this symbol has the same hold over people that it exercised 3,000 years ago.

PLACES TO VISIT

Rocky Valley carvings, Cornwall

Location: Rocky Valley is a mile north-east of Tintagel, off the B3263, and the two carvings are on a rock face behind a ruined building. (SX 073894)

Such carvings as these are impossible to date, and the suggested dates for these range from 1500 BC to the seventeenth century AD! Or they may date from early Christian times, when there was an influx of Celtic missionaries into Cornwall; the retreat of St Nectan was in the upper part of Rocky Valley. The two mazes are of Cretan design, and show little wear, but the rock is a hard slate and well sheltered.

Rocky Valley carvings.

Few maze rock carvings or drawings have been discovered in Britain or Ireland. At Rockshaw Quarry (Surrey) five Cretan labyrinths were chalked on to the rock face, possibly in the seventeenth or eighteenth centuries by miners. The so-called Hollywood Stone in Ireland carries a true rock-carving of a maze, possibly dating from early Christian times. It was found beside a pilgrims' track in the Wicklow Mountains; it is now in the National Museum of Ireland.

Turf maze at Hilton, Cambridgeshire

Location: Hilton is 4 miles south-east of Huntingdon, and the maze is on the village green, not far from the church. (TL 293663)

The obelisk in the centre of this well-kept maze states that it was cut in 1660 by 19-year-old William Sparrow, but it is more likely that he was recutting an earlier maze which had been neglected. Again, nothing is known of its history apart from this enigmatic message.

200

Four mazes at Alkborough, Humberside

Hilton turf maze.

Location: Alkborough is 6 miles north of Scunthorpe, and the turf maze is on the western side of the village, overlooking the plain of the River Trent. (SE 880218)

The turf maze is known as Julian's Bower, and probably dates from the early thirteenth century when a cell of Benedictine monks was based at Alkborough. Not far away to the south is a square earthwork called the Countess Close, date and purpose unknown. Julian's Bower was in use at least until the beginning of the nineteenth century, when the villagers played May-Eve games there, 'under an indefinite persuasion of something unseen and unknown co-operating with them'.

The design of the turf maze can be seen elsewhere in the village. In the church a maze has been set into the porch floor, and a small maze can also be seen in the stained glass of the east window. In the cemetery (to the south of the village) can be found a tombstone with a maze on a brass plate, illustrated on page 202.

201

Turf maze near Brandsby, North Yorkshire

Alkborough maze.

Location: In the Howardian Hills 10 miles west of Malton; the maze is on the grass verge of a lane between Brandsby and Dalby. (SE 625719)

This 'City of Troy' is the smallest surviving turf maze, measuring 26 by 22 feet. Its original location was some yards to the west, the original site having been destroyed by carts using the grass verge. It has been recut several times, but is now kept in good condition.

Nine Men's Morris, Finchingfield, Essex

Location: Carved on a windowsill in Finchingfield church, 10 miles south-east of Saffron Walden. (TL 686328)

Nine Men's Morris is a game of great antiquity, once very popular in Britain. The square outline was cut in turf, chalked on floors, carved on tables, seats, church windowsills – anywhere where people gathered together. It was also called 'Siege of Troy' and 'The Troy Game', and the layout is an elementary labyrinth. The object of this game for two players was for each

Nine Men's Morris.

203

player to get three of his nine counters in a row on the intersections of the lines or in the three angles of one corner.

Another name for Nine Men's Morris was merrils, similar to the old French name for hopscotch, *jeu de merelles*, and hopscotch itself may have been derived from maze dances. One researcher, Frederick Hirsch, believes that children's pavement games like hopscotch are a folk-memory of pre-Christian cosmologies. He says that the game symbolises the course of the sun, and in support of this theory reports that Danish children cry 'one year old' or 'I have a year' after having completed one course of the hopscotch figure according to the children's rules. Roger Caillois confirms the antiquity of hopscotch when he says: 'Hopscotch indeed symbolized the labyrinth through which the initiate must first wander' and 'In antiquity, hopscotch was a labyrinth in which one pushed a stone – i.e. the soul – toward the exit.' In Cornwall the spiral form of hopscotch was called 'snail-creep', reminding us of the spiral dance 'snails' creep' described earlier.

Hedge maze in Glendurgan Garden, Cornwall

Location: 3 miles south-west of Falmouth. (SW 772277)

Hedge maze in Glendurgan Garden.

This beautiful valley garden is in the care of the National Trust and is open to the public from March to October. It is well

worth a visit, especially the fine laurel hedge maze, planted in
1833. The hedges are tall and the pathway narrow, so it is quite
a frightening experience to enter this maze, especially when you
get lost!

There are about sixteen hedge mazes in Britain which are
worth visiting, including those at Somerleyton Hall near Lowestoft (Suffolk), Hever Castle, Edenbridge (Kent), Hazlehead
Park, Aberdeen (Grampian Region), Tatton Park, Knutsford
(Cheshire), and Blackgang Chine (Isle of Wight).

Maze tombstone in Hadstock churchyard, Essex

Location: 5 miles north-east of Saffron Walden. (TL 558448)

The stone marking the grave of Michael Ayrton (1921–1975)
appropriately carries a labyrinth design. Michael Ayrton was an
artist, sculptor and writer, whose novel *The Maze Maker*
describing the life of Daedalus should be read by everyone
interested in the imagery of the maze. In 1969 Michael Ayrton
created a maze at Arkville, New York State, USA, which was
constructed of stone and brick walls 10 feet high, 200,000 bricks
being used. The two central chambers contain bronzes by
Michael Ayrton, of the Minotaur, and of Daedalus and Icarus.
Another bronze of the Minotaur can also be seen in Postman's
Park near St Paul's in London.

Anyone visiting Michael Ayrton's grave should also explore
Hadstock church, for it is of Saxon origin with several interest-
ing features, including several Saxon windows and a unique
Saxon door.

Hadstock gravestone.

17. *Giants, devils and living stones*

We are today largely an urban population, whereas our ancestors were country dwellers, many people never travelling far from home throughout the whole of their lives. Today we are also a shifting population, moving temporarily or permanently from one area to another without much concern. In the past the people were rooted in their local environment almost as firmly as the trees in the ground, and it would need a great upheaval to move them away to another district. They also moved around largely on foot, and in that way acquired a far more intimate knowledge of their own locality than we can today, travelling in cars which effectively cut us off from the outside world. Every tree, stone, mound, stream, river, pool, hill, had its place in their environment, and the most unusual features became the focus of tales 'explaining' how they came to be there. We have already written about Rudston monolith (Humberside) being thrown at the church by the Devil (Chapter 4), and some sites, like the Devil's Arrows (North Yorkshire), carry the outline of their story in their name. Many standing stones were given 'Devil' names, perhaps at a time when Christianity became the predominant religion and many of the earlier sacred sites came to be regarded as the haunt of the Devil. In areas of Scandinavian and Saxon influence, names like Grim, Thor and Woden were sometimes used, as in Grimes Graves (Norfolk).

Most Devil sites are in England, particularly the south, with a few in Wales and Scotland, whereas places attributed to giants are largely in the west, with very few in central and eastern England but many in Cornwall and north Wales. Many standing stones were traditionally attributed to giants, also sizeable burial chambers, and earthworks which had obviously needed great earth-moving efforts in their construction. The name of the hillfort Tre'r Ceiri (Gwynedd) translates as 'town of the giants', and Barclodiad-y-Gawres, a passage-grave on Anglesey (Gwynedd), means 'the giantess's apronful', referring to her having collected an apronful of stones to build the mound.

206

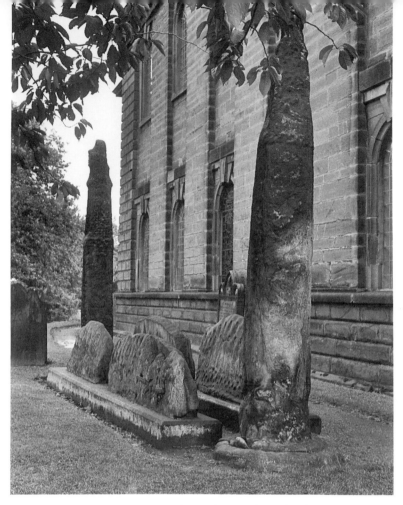

The Giant's Grave in Penrith churchyard (Cumbria), in reality two worn crosses dating from around 1000 and some hogback gravestones. In the same churchyard is a wheel-headed cross called the Giant's Thumb. These names are thought to commemorate a tenth-century king who became a legendary hero or giant in local lore.

Since the twelfth century, Stonehenge has also been called the Giants' Dance in some quarters, and the mighty stones of Callanish (Western Isles) were said to be giants turned to stone for refusing to embrace the Christian religion.

Ancient sites (usually cairns or barrows) were often believed to be fairy haunts, and they were said to dance or make music there. Willy Howe (Humberside) is a prominent round barrow which housed a fairy dwelling, seen by a drunken villager late one night. He heard people singing and went to see who it was. Through an open door in the side of the mound he could see people banqueting at large tables. One of the people saw him and offered him a cup. He took it but threw away the contents, not wishing to come under the spell of the fairies, and ran off with the goblet, which was made of an unknown material. This tale was recorded by William of Newburgh in the twelfth century. Another tale told of people digging into the mound and finding a golden chest. They tried to pull it out with horses,

207

but it sank back into the mound and no one has ever been able to recover it.

The fairies would sometimes help people by mending broken tools, or would give a reward when helped by humans. In Welsh folklore stories telling of people who saw the fairies are very common and some are presented as factual rather than fictional. Indeed, people still claim to see the fairies, or 'Little People', and these witnesses appear to be neither liars nor insane! Perhaps the Little People do still live among us, like the monsters and ghosts we shall describe in Chapter 20.

Famous people, both real and imaginary, were sometimes associated with ancient sites. We have already described in Chapter 14 the use of King Arthur's name at places said to have been visited by him. Other heroes similarly remembered include Sir Bevis of Hampton in southern England (e.g. Bevis's Thumb long barrow in West Sussex), Wayland the Smith (e.g. Wayland's Smithy, Oxfordshire – see Chapter 2), Jack o' Kent in Herefordshire and Gwent, Michael Scot in northern England and southern Scotland, Robin Hood and Little John in Nottinghamshire, and Oliver Cromwell (e.g. Oliver Cromwell's Hill at Eye in Suffolk).

Because of their air of mystery, and there being no obvious reason for their construction, prehistoric sites have become a focus for a rich and varied folklore. Standing stones and stone circles were sometimes said to be people turned to stone, often for dancing on a Sunday, such as the Merry Maidens stone circle (Cornwall) with the Pipers standing stones close by, and the stone circles at Stanton Drew (Avon); or for working in the fields on a Sunday (the Duddo Stones, Northumberland), or for playing the game of hurling on a Sunday (the Hurlers stone circles, Cornwall), and other similar religious transgressions. Some stones were said to move or go to a nearby stream to drink when they heard the clock strike twelve, or the cock crow, or sometimes on a special day in the year, like the Hoar Stone at Enstone (Oxfordshire) which goes to drink on Midsummer Eve. Some stones were believed to have the power to return if taken away from their rightful place, like a stone on Cefn Carn Cafall (Powys), said to bear the hoofmark of King Arthur's horse Cafall, and which would come back of its own accord if carried away. At a number of stone circles the stones were believed to be uncountable – this was said of Stonehenge, the Rollright Stones, Long Meg and Her Daughters, the Callanish Stones. The same story was told of a few chambered tombs, and when folklorist Leslie Grinsell visited the Countless Stones

208

near Aylesford (Kent) in the late 1940s, he found numbers chalked on to the stones, showing that the tradition was still alive.

Prehistoric sites were often believed to have healing properties and these sites were regularly visited by the sick who performed the necessary rituals and thus hoped to be cured. Stonehenge was one such site, as recorded by Geoffrey of Monmouth in the twelfth century:

> For in these stones is a mystery, and a healing virtue against many ailments ... for they washed the stones and poured the water into baths, whereby those who were sick were cured. Moreover, they mixed confections of herbs with the water, whereby those who were wounded were healed, for not a stone is there that is wanting in virtue or leech-craft.

People would crawl through holed stones like the Men-an-Tol (Cornwall), or pass clothing through smaller holes in stones, as pregnant women did in Ireland in order to ensure a safe childbirth. At the Toothie Stane in Argyll, people with toothache would go and knock a nail or screw into one of the stones of this chambered tomb and expect to gain relief from their pain.

Such practices may have developed as a result of people's awe at these strange monuments, but there are other customs which strongly suggest that the rituals originally performed at prehistoric sites had been handed down through the generations, although in a greatly degenerate form. On Orkney sick people would walk round the Stones of Stenness three times with the sun (deasil) and such circumambulation rituals were practised elsewhere, for example at holy wells (as described in more detail in our book *Sacred Waters*), and sometimes even at Christian churches! In 1650 the Synod of Argyll was trying to stop people walking 'sungates' around the church before going in for divine service.

Whether or not these customs were derived from prehistoric rituals, it is clear that the people of later centuries were much in awe of the prehistoric remains, so much so that they believed it was dangerous to interfere with them, and this belief may well have helped to preserve them to the present day. Anyone digging into a barrow could expect retribution of some kind, and it often came in the form of a thunderstorm, or a ghost, or ill health or bad luck thereafter following the offender and his family. In 1859 a farmer on the Isle of Man opened a barrow on his land and then sacrificed a heifer in order to prevent the retribution which he clearly expected.

Apart from prehistoric sites, other landscape features were also rich in folklore, such as hills (see the Wrekin in 'Places to Visit') and bridges (see the Devil's Bridge in 'Places to Visit'), and the lore even extended offshore, in those areas where the sea has in previous centuries inundated the land. This has happened within living memory at Dunwich on the Suffolk coast, and indeed is still happening. The church bells are said to be heard ringing from time to time, from beneath the waves. Off the west and north coasts of Wales are said to be areas where the sea has drowned the land, such as Cantre 'r Gwaelod, a fertile stretch of land 40 miles long between the Teifi and Bardsey Island, which was defended from the sea by an embankment and sluices. According to the legend, one night in the fifth century when the keeper of the embankment was drunk, he left the sluices open and the sea broke through, only a few inhabitants of the sixteen cities surviving. When the sea is still, it is said that the remains of buildings can be seen through the clear water, and in rough weather the church bells can be heard. Most famous of these sunken lands is of course Lyonesse, said to have extended west from Cornwall as far as the Scilly Isles. It was drowned by the sea in an immense cataclysm in the distant past, a few projecting rocks being all that can now be seen above the surface.

This brief introduction hardly does justice to the wealth of

The Cornish coast at Land's End, where once lay the now-legendary land of Lyonesse.

folklore throughout Britain and Ireland. A much more detailed coverage of the folklore of ancient sites will be found in our earlier book *The Secret Country*, and also in Leslie V. Grinsell's comprehensive gazetteer, *Folklore of Prehistoric Sites in Britain*.

PLACES TO VISIT

St Levan Stone, Cornwall

Location: In the churchyard at St Levan, which is on the south Cornish coast, 7 miles south-west of Penzance. (SW 380223)

This rock by the church porch was said to have been St Levan's resting place when he returned from fishing trips. He is supposed to have split it open by striking it with his fist and saying:

> When with panniers astride
> A pack-horse one can ride
> Through St Levan's Stone,
> The world will be done.

Fortunately it is nowhere near wide enough yet for anyone to start worrying!

St Levan Stone.

Caractacus Stone, Somerset

Location: On Winsford Hill, Exmoor, 4 miles north-west of
Dulverton. (SS 890335)

Here is an example of divine retribution as a result of disturbing
an ancient stone. Excited by rumours of treasure buried
beneath this stone, a waggoner hitched his team of horses to the
stone to try and uproot it. But it overturned his waggon and
horses and crushed him. Now they are all said to haunt the spot
on foggy nights.

Gelert's Grave, Gwynedd

Location: At Beddgelert, 11 miles south-east of Caernarfon,
along a path by the river. (SH 591478)

Gelert was the favourite hound of Prince Llywelyn the Great,
and the legend tells how the Prince returned from hunting one
day to be met by Gelert, his jaws dripping with blood. The
Prince rushed into the nursery and could not find his baby son.
The room was disordered and bloody, and assuming the worst
the Prince stabbed Gelert with his sword. As the dog died a
loud wailing could be heard, and the Prince found his child
beneath the upturned cradle, beside the body of a huge wolf
which had been killed by Gelert. Broken-hearted, the Prince
buried Gelert beneath a cairn, the place now marked by a slab
upon which the story is engraved. In fact this is an old tale,
known in many parts of the world, and it would seem that it was
adapted to fit local conditions only two hundred years ago. The
place was then called Beth Kellarth or Kelert, probably after a
Celtic saint. The name 'Gelert' was invented, to make the
similar but new name of Beddgelert, Gelert's Grave. This local
legend was concocted, and the 'grave' built, in order to boost
trade. It was certainly successful: today thousands of people
visit Gelert's Grave every year.

The Druid Stone, Bungay, Suffolk

Location: In St Mary's churchyard, in the town centre, which is
on the Suffolk/Norfolk border, 11 miles west of Lowestoft.
(TM 338897)

This rounded boulder close to the church porch was believed to
be a channel of communication with the Devil. All that was

212

necessary to get him to appear was to knock on the stone twelve times, or to run around it twelve times.

Llyn y Dywarchen, Gwynedd

Location: 7 miles south-east of Caernarfon, close to the B4418 north-west of Rhyd-Ddu. (SH 5653)

The name of this lake means 'Lake of the Sod', which refers to a small island which used to float about on the water. Giraldus Cambrensis writing in the twelfth century described it in his *Journey Through Wales*: 'On the highest parts of these mountains are two lakes worthy of admiration. The one has a floating island in it, which is often driven from one side to the other by the force of the winds; and the shepherds behold with astonishment their cattle, whilst feeding, carried to the distant parts of the lake.' Local people believed that 'if it floated towards the north the markets would rise, if to the south they would fall.'

This area north-west of Beddgelert used to be known as the Land of the Fairies, and their music could often be heard at night. There was a fairy dwelling underneath the lake, and one day a young man from a nearby farm happened to see one of the fairy girls. He fell in love with her, and they were married, but only on condition that she was never touched by iron. Several years later, she was accidentally touched by her stirrup-iron while out riding, and was fetched away home by her family. It was said, though, that she used to stand on the floating island in the lake and from there would talk for hours to her ex-husband on the shore.

Mermaid at Zennor, Cornwall

Location: On a bench-end inside Zennor church, which is 5 miles north of Penzance. (SW 455385)

This fifteenth-century bench-end carving is said to depict a local mermaid who was enticed out of the sea by the beautiful singing of a chorister at the church. She lured him into the sea, and he was never seen again. There are variations on this story, which probably evolved to explain the old carving, rather than the carving commemorating the legend. Mermaid legends are familiar at other places all around the British coastline, and even some inland pools are reputed to be their homes. There are even a few factual reports of mermaids being seen just offshore, but the more prosaic commentators have explained these sightings away as seals or mirages.

Zennor mermaid.

214

Devil's Bridge, Dyfed

Devil's Bridge.

Location: At the small village of Devil's Bridge, 10 miles east-south-east of Aberystwyth; the bridge is crossed by the A4120 and is best seen from down below at river level. (SN 742770)

There are really three bridges here above each other, crossing the River Mynach where it runs through a deep gorge. The lowest of the three was built by the Devil, according to legend. He saw that an old woman's cow was stranded on the wrong side of the gorge and said he would build her a bridge if he could become the owner of the first living creature to use it. She agreed, but when the bridge was completed she threw a piece of bread over, which was chased by her dog, and the Devil was outwitted. In another version of this tale, the Devil built the bridge for the farmers and shepherds, who had been unable to

215

persuade the rich monks of Strata Florida to build it for them. He again asked for the sacrifice of the first creatures to cross, thinking these would be the many people anxious to use the bridge and thus unwittingly provide him with souls, but the old woman outsmarted him as in the other story. She was one of the monks in disguise!

Little John's Grave, Derbyshire

Location: In Hathersage churchyard, 8 miles south-west of Sheffield city centre. (SK 234818)

There are strong local traditions connecting this area with Robin Hood and his Merry Men, including place names like Robin Hood's Moss, Robin Hood Croft, Robin Hood's Cave and Robin Hood's Well, all close to Hathersage. In the churchyard of St Michael and All Angels at Hathersage is a grave claimed to be that of Robin Hood's lieutenant, Little John, but no one is really sure whose grave it is, or even, of course, whether Robin Hood and Little John ever existed. The grave was opened in 1784 and six feet down a gigantic human thigh bone was found, 32 inches long. The man whose bone it

Little John's Grave.

was would have been 7 feet tall. Captain James Shuttleworth, who had ordered the grave to be opened, was told that 'No good will come of it', but he laughed and hung the bone above his bed. Shortly afterwards he suffered a series of accidents, and eventually the bone was reburied. Also at Hathersage, the cottage where Little John was said to have died stood near the church until the last century; and there were once also a cap and long-bow in the church, said to have been Little John's.

The Wrekin, Shropshire

Location: This prominent hill over 1,300 feet high can be seen from miles around. It is 8 miles south-east of Shrewsbury, and can be most easily climbed from the north-east side.

The Wrekin has several interesting features, but first the legend of its formation. It was attributed to a giant, but its construction was accidental: a giant with a grudge against the people of Shrewsbury set out with a spadeful of earth, intending to dam the River Severn and flood the town. But he became lost and was forced to ask the way of a cobbler he met near Wellington. He explained why he needed to reach Shrewsbury, and the

The Wrekin.

quick-witted cobbler, who was carrying a sackful of shoes for repair, told the giant that Shrewsbury was so far away, he had worn out all these shoes since leaving the town. The giant, feeling tired and disheartened, dumped his load of earth and so the Wrekin was formed. The earth he scraped off his boots made another sizeable hill close by, now called the Ercall.

There was once an Iron Age hillfort on the summit of the Wrekin, but few traces are now visible. The names Hell Gate and Heaven Gate on the hill are said to refer to civil war battles. The Needle's Eye is a cleft in the rock on the summit, said to have been formed at the Crucifixion when the rocks were torn asunder. It is just possible for an active person to climb through it, and girls used to do this, taking care not to look back else they would never be married. Their boyfriends met them with a kiss on the other side. This ritual has hints of a fertility custom, but its age is not known. Also on the summit is the Raven's Bowl or Cuckoo's Cup, a hollow in a rock which is said to be always full of water though it is not fed by a spring. There was also (and maybe still is) a holy well on the Wrekin, St Hawthorn's Well, whose water was reputed to be good for skin diseases. Sufferers had to drink the water and bathe the afflicted part in it before sunrise.

18. *The turning year: customs and traditions*

Throughout the year in Britain a regular succession of festivals and customs is still practised. Some are of recent origin, perhaps only two or three hundred years old, but others can be traced back to our pre-Christian heritage and mark the high points of the turning year with its changing seasons. For us the year ends with Christmastime, which together with New Year's Eve makes up our midwinter season of festivities. But for the people who inhabited Britain before Christianity came, the year started with the onset of winter and was marked by the Celtic fire festival of Samhain which by our present calendar falls on 1 November. From this time we have inherited Hallowe'en (31 October), the last night of the old year when the barrier between this world and the world of spirits is temporarily dissolved, the dead can walk abroad, and by enacting the appropriate ritual future events can be foreseen.

Until the early years of this century many areas still lit their huge hilltop fires at Samhain. There the crowds would gather and the young people jump across the crackling logs, and later the ashes would be scattered across the fields to purify them, while a blazing branch was run around the boundaries to bless them and ensure a good harvest in the coming year. Often an effigy called the hag or witch and representing the woes of the past year was hurled on to the blaze, purging the community of past failures and clearing the way for a fresh start to the new year. Little now remains of this life-giving festival other than the bonfire and fireworks of 5 November. After the attempt to blow up Parliament in 1605 the remaining Samhain fire festivities were adapted to commemorate this date. Nearly four centuries later the religious and political implications are generally forgotten, and it is the fascination of the living elemental fire which now draws people to the celebrations.

Then followed the annual fire ceremony on the midwinter solstice, 21 December being the shortest day of the year. This fire was kindled inside the house and central to it was the Yule

219

Log which was ceremoniously brought in, decorated with greenery and dowsed with libations of ale. For twelve days it slowly burnt in the hearth, whilst games and contests were held amidst the feasting and drinking. The unburnt portion was kept as a talisman against lightning and fire, or was steeped in water which when drunk by cattle would assist them in giving birth, and the ashes were scattered on the fields to promote a good harvest. At this time too, the house interior was decorated with greenery, holly and ivy and some laurel and pine boughs. The mysterious mistletoe was used too, though being harder to find it was less dominant than the others. The origin of the custom of kissing beneath it is unknown, though a connection with fertility ritual seems very probable. Today's ubiquitous Christmas tree is of comparatively recent origin in Britain, having been introduced by German immigrants in the mid-nineteenth century, but nevertheless fitting in with the earlier custom of decorating the home with greenery.

This midwinter ceremony was not of Celtic origin but has come to us through our Saxon and Scandinavian forebears and it occurred in various forms over much of northern Europe. It

Christmas Mummers at Symondsbury (Dorset) photographed in 1952.

celebrated the dormant but ever-present life-force in nature and reaffirmed the promise of the resurgent springtime. In the fourth century the Church adopted the midwinter festivities and designated 25 December as the birthday of Jesus Christ, although the actual date is of course unknown. Some of the Christmas fun was provided by the Mummers who enacted a short drama, the principal characters being St George, the Dragon or a Turkish Knight, and the Doctor. Usually after a fight St George lies fatally wounded but is restored to life by the doctor's magic potion. Again the theme here is death and regeneration. Other characters and local variations were introduced to add to the fun and interest, but the age-old underlying theme remained the same. In the apple-growing areas of the West Country the orchards were wassailed at this season. At night cider was poured on to the tree roots while the wassail song was sung, then guns were fired into the branches to scare away the evil spirits and to reawaken the trees to a fruitful season's growth.

The New Year is seen in, in the north of England and in Scotland, by 'First Footing'. Ideally a handsome dark-haired male should be the first to cross the threshold into the house, carrying bread, salt, coal and money, symbolising food, warmth and prosperity for the coming year. In return he is welcomed with food and drink. In Wales and the West Country 1 January would see the children calling on neighbours with 'calennig', singing a verse as they held a decorated apple, and they would receive a gift of food or money. Another custom still practised at the turn of the century in South Wales on 1 January was the sprinkling of water throughout the house and over its occupants by local youths. All of these New Year customs were intended to bring good fortune and fertility, and we have dealt with this theme at greater length in our earlier book *Earth Rites*.

Some time in February or March falls the Movable Feast of Shrove Tuesday when the traditional pancake race is held. Originally the women made pancakes so that all the butter and eggs were used before the frugal observances of Lent must begin. How they came to run a race to the church carrying their frying pans and tossing the pancake three times on the way is unknown. At one time there were many Shrove Tuesday football games and a few are still played. These are not the type of football played countrywide on sports fields every winter Saturday, but a riotous mêlée of humanity which surges up and down the town's streets and out across the fields. By the last century they had become so uncontrollably violent that many

221

were suppressed by local authorities with the aid of the police or even armed troops. At Scarborough (North Yorkshire) the afternoon of Shrove Tuesday is devoted to skipping, when all ages and both sexes gather on the front to skip in groups, and this continues until dusk.

Some time between 22 March and 25 April falls Easter, originally the festival of the Saxon spring goddess Eostre, and in the fourth century adopted by the Church to celebrate the resurrection of Christ. Eostre's totem creature was the hare, who has latterly degenerated into the Easter Bunny, and her gift was the egg, symbolic of emerging life. So eggs play a dominant part in the Easter customs when traditionally pace (a corruption of 'paschal', meaning Passover) eggs were made by hardboiling eggs which were then dyed multi-colours by being bound with bark and leaves, or hand-painted in brilliant colours and hidden in house and garden for the children to find. It was traditional for groups of young men to call at houses to enact the Pace Egg Play, which was similar to the mummers' play, and to be rewarded with gifts of eggs. Later this was abbreviated into a short begging verse, but today little of it remains. The only activity now, principally in northern England and Scotland, is the pastime of rolling the coloured eggs down a slope until the shells crack, when they are eaten.

On Easter Monday at Hallaton (Leicestershire) the men of that village meet those of nearby Medbourne in a 'Bottle Kicking' contest, but first a large meat pie known as Hare Pie is divided up and thrown to the crowd to be scrambled for. The 'bottles' in the contest are three small barrels which are paraded through the village and then kicked or manhandled by the opposing teams towards their own territory, all of which appears to be another variant of the Shrove Tuesday football games.

Nowadays May Day, 1 May, is only a pale reflection of what it once was. Considered by the Celts to be the first day of summer, throughout the centuries the Beltane festivities which celebrate the upsurging fertility of the land have always been particularly joyful and colourful. Traditionally the young people spent the previous night in the woods and with the dawn they returned to the town or village to deck out the streets and houses with greenery and may blossom. The maypole was a focal point of the festivities and was often a permanent fixture, being 70 or 80 feet high and painted red and white, symbolic of fertility and a fresh beginning. The festivities were presided over by a May Queen and King, and sports, dancing, eating and drinking filled the rest of the day. One of the few remaining permanent maypoles is at Barwick in Elmet (West Yorkshire). It is 86 feet tall and is lowered and refurbished every three years.

At many local May Day celebrations the children dance prettily and weave coloured sashes around a little post, but the current of pagan life-forces is now absent – Nature (with a capital 'N') has been exorcised. One ceremony where some of the original vitality may still be experienced is at Padstow in Cornwall. Every May Day the 'Obby 'Oss, a menacing black figure, circulates in the streets with its attendant musicians and dancers swaying and weaving to the simple and haunting music. When the 'Oss jumps towards a young woman and covers her with its skirt, within twelve months she will if unmarried have a husband, or if married then will have a baby, so potent is the 'Oss's fertilising power. At nearby Helston on 8 May the Furry Dance is held, when elegantly attired couples dance along the streets and in and out of the houses, accompanied by the town band. This custom is thought to be one of the oldest surviving relics of communal festivals which celebrated the return of summer.

Whitsuntide falls at the end of May, and this is the time in which the Morris dancers are much in evidence, although they may be seen at any time during the spring and summer months. Dressed in white, adorned with brightly coloured scarves and ribbons and wearing small bells strapped to their legs, they pace

The Kennet Morris Men from Reading (Berkshire) here dancing in July 1982 at Much Wenlock (Shropshire).

out their intricate measures to the jaunty rhythms of traditional country tunes often played on fiddle and accordion. Their traditional home is in the Midland counties with strongholds in Oxfordshire and Essex, the team from Bampton claiming a continuous tradition of five hundred years, though elsewhere they have been disbanded and later revived as local interest waxed and waned. The meaning and origin of the Morris dances are unknown, but there can be little doubt that they were originally directed towards promoting the fertility of crops and cattle. This is one traditional custom which is very much on the increase, as interest in Morris dancing grows and more teams are formed.

Another traditional Whitsun practice with ancient connections occurs at Cooper's Hill, Birdlip (Gloucestershire) where cheeses are rolled down the steep slope, chased by the local youths. Although the mundane reason for this ritual is said to be the retention of the grazing rights on the hill, it has obvious sunwheel symbolism and stems from the same impulse as the flaming cartwheels bound with straw and pitch which were bowled downhill in the Vale of Glamorgan on Midsummer Day.

The summer solstice falls on 21 June and three days later is Midsummer Day. In past ages Midsummer Eve would have been ablaze with the lights of great fires lit upon the sacred high points of the land. People would leap across the flames and cattle were driven between fires to give them good health. Later, glowing embers were scattered across the fields to promote fertility. Nothing of this remains except at Whalton in Northumberland, where, having ignored the alteration to the calendar in 1752, the people celebrate Midsummer on 4 July, Old Midsummer Eve, with dancing around a Baal fire on the green, and this has occurred for at least two hundred years. A 1920 revival has brought back some of the Midsummer fires to Cornwall where once more fires blaze from the hilltops and invocations for health, prosperity and fertility are made in the old Cornish language.

On the second Friday in August a figure of menacing appearance walks the streets of South Queensferry, by the Firth of Forth (West Lothian). He is the Burryman and from head to foot he is covered in thistle burrs, which stick steadfastly to him. Even his face is covered with burrs, holes being left only for eyes and nose. On his head his hat is covered with seventy roses and one dahlia and he wears four roses on his front and four on his back. With two assistants who carry flower-decorated staves he silently parades the town's boundaries, speaking to no one and giving no thanks when donations are placed in the collectors' boxes. But even so he is welcomed by all the townspeople. What does the Burryman represent and what is his origin? No one knows; the meaning of this ceremony is lost in antiquity. Some theorise that he commemorates the landing of Queen Margaret from whence the town gets its name, but other herring fishing towns along the coast also had their Burryman in earlier centuries. Is he a 'green man' or a fishing harvest fertility figure, or is he perhaps a 'scapegoat' figure who at one time had burrs thrown at him by the people to represent the ridding of their sins of the past year? Probably we will now never know his real significance.

Another enigmatic ceremony occurs annually in early September at Abbots Bromley (Staffordshire). Here six male dancers carry sets of reindeer antlers in a twenty-mile circuit of the area, stopping at various farms and houses to perform their archaic routine. They are accompanied by six other figures, the Hobby Horse, Maid Marian (a man dressed as a woman and carrying a collecting ladle), a Fool, a Bowman and a triangle and accordion player. They form two lines, dance towards each other and back away again several times before passing with a dextrous twist of the antlers and then form a single file to circle and weave before the next confrontation. How long the antlers have been used in the dance is unknown, as indeed are the age and origin of the dance itself, but there is little doubt of their fertility implications and probable connection with a Celtic horned god cult.

Traditionally the high point of the agricultural year was the successful gathering and safe storage of the harvest, and in past ages there were many customs to be observed before the final celebration of the Harvest Supper. With the present mechanisation of farming and the disbanding of the farming community the customs have been largely forgotten and the significance of 'Harvest Home' greatly diminished. In some areas the Harvest Supper is still held, but there can rarely be the same air of triumphant celebration that was evident in the past. The church service of Harvest Festival is widely practised but is of no great antiquity, having been introduced in 1843 by R. S. Hawker, the vicar of Morwenstowe in Cornwall. It is second only to the Christmas service in popularity and this indicates a deep need for people to acknowledge and give thanks for the sustaining seasonal cycle.

When the corn was reaped by hand sickle, it was considered

ill luck to cut the last sheaf or 'neck' for it contained the Corn Spirit which would then be killed. One after another the reapers would throw their sickles until the 'neck' was cut, thus sharing the responsibility. If one individual's sickle was seen to give the definitive cut, then he received special attention in some districts and would have the best seat at the Harvest Supper, but in others he received a jostling and roughing-up in the field, the suggestion being that in times of antiquity there would have been a living sacrifice which would restore the vitality of the Corn Spirit. Often the neck was held high with customary shouts of triumph by the workers and one of them would race with it to the farmhouse, there to be repelled by the women who threw water over him. Sometimes the neck was borne back in triumph on top of the last load of corn sheaves, where again water, as a sign of future fertility, would be splashed over it.

The practices attached to the last sheaf varied from region to region and are too numerous to detail here, but often it was kept somewhere in the house and used in some way the following year, either being mixed with the seed corn, ploughed into the soil, burnt after the following harvest, or fed to the best beast. It might even be left to grow and rot away without being cut. It also provided the material for making the Corn Dolly or Kern Baby, or in a poor harvest the Old Woman or Cailleach. This could be in the form of a figure with head and hands of wheat ears and wearing a paper dress or in one of the more familiar geometric designs, a spiral, a pyramid, a cage or feather shape. Today the art of the Corn Dolly flourishes and finely made examples can be bought in many craft shops, but they are no longer seen in the fields at harvest-time and the Corn Spirit is now a stranger in the land.

In 'Places to Visit' we describe just a few of the many traditional customs which still actively celebrate the different facets of the turning year.

PLACES TO VISIT

Padstow 'Obby 'Oss, Cornwall

Date: 1 May
Location: Padstow is on the north Cornish coast, 10 miles north-west of Bodmin.

May Day begins early in Padstow, for during the previous night the mayers go around the town, singing the Night Song outside the houses of prominent residents. One verse runs, for example,

> Rise up, Mrs ——, all in your gown of green,
> For summer is I-comen in today.
> You are as fair a lady as waits upon the Queen,
> In the merry month of May.

The Teaser, with his baton in his right hand, dancing with the 'Obby 'Oss at Padstow on 1 May 1978.

Next morning the festivities start in earnest, when the two 'Osses begin to tour the town separately with their accompanying teams of dancers. Each 'Oss is led by a Teaser, who carries a club or baton and dances with the 'Oss. Everyone sings the customary song and every so often the 'Oss 'dies', to suddenly revive and move on around the town. Until about 1930 there was also a ceremony at Treator Pool, where the 'Oss drank the water and sprinkled his followers, possibly enacting an ancient rain-making ceremony. The 'Oss still chases the girls, and to be caught by him and covered by his 'skirt' signifies a baby or a husband, depending on the girl's status. The dancing continues until late afternoon, when the two 'Osses meet at the maypole in the market square.

This festival is understandably popular, and each year the small town with its narrow streets is packed with visitors. The hypnotic music is very compelling, and this still earthy ceremony gives a glimpse into how the traditional customs had such a hold over people and were so popular. To be at Padstow on May Day, or at any similar ancient ceremony, is to understand why such pursuits, apparently so alien to the twentieth-century ethos, refuse to die. They appeal to everyone's basic needs and instincts, and provide us all with a means of expressing our relationship with the life force, so sadly absent from today's slick modern entertainments.

Well-dressing – at several places in England, but especially in Derbyshire

Date: May–August

From the earliest times rural communities have treated their sources of water with respect and veneration, and by decorating a local spring or well the people would honour the guardian spirit of the water source. Today in Derbyshire the tradition is still practised but the decoration has evolved from a simple garland to very elaborate and large pictures. These are made by pressing flower petals on to a surface of wet clay on a board, also leaves, berries, cones, bark, moss, pebbles – any naturally found object may be used to form the picture and the words, which usually have a religious theme such as a biblical verse or depiction of a famous cathedral. These well-dressings can be seen throughout the summer at different towns and villages in Derbyshire. During May: Etwall, Wirksworth, Tissington; during June: Monyash, Ashford-in-the-Water, Hope, Tides-

Well-dressing at Youlgreave, June 1982.

228

FOLLOW ME

well, Litton, Buxton, Youlgreave, Breaston, Rowsley, Edlaston, Bakewell; during July: Dore, Whitwell, Pilsley, Stoney Middleton, Ault Hucknall, Holmewood and Heath, Bonsall; during August: Bradwell, Barlow. Check the exact dates, which vary from year to year, with the local tourist information centre.

Lewes Bonfire Night Celebrations, East Sussex

Date: 5 November
Location: Lewes is 6 miles north-east of Brighton.

On 5 November or Guy Fawkes Day we are celebrating the discovery of the Gunpowder Plot in 1605, when a group of men laid gunpowder in the cellars of the Palace of Westminster in London with the intention of destroying the King and the Houses of Lords and Commons, all of whom would be assembled for the Opening of Parliament. Guy Fawkes was the man chosen to light the fuse, but the authorities were 'tipped off' and he was arrested on 5 November.

This Catholic-inspired plot caused an upsurge of anti-Catholic feeling throughout the country, which is still retained in the Lewes ceremony, probably because during the reign of Mary I, seventeen Protestants were burnt there as heretics. Until recently, an effigy of the Pope was burnt along with one of Guy Fawkes. There are several separate torchlit processions at Lewes, each representing a different Bonfire Society, with the participants in fancy dress, and one of them appears as the Pope. During the last century huge fires were lit in the town centre and lighted tar-barrels rolled through the streets, the whole occasion being potentially very dangerous, and rioting ensued when the authorities tried to stop the celebrations altogether, so a safer compromise was worked out, and the celebrations thrive today.

Elsewhere in Britain, of course, thousands of local bonfires are lit on 5 November, ranging from the small garden bonfires attended by a single family, to the huge municipal events. Nearly four hundred years after the Gunpowder Plot the central events are still remembered in the effigies of Guy Fawkes which are made by children and burned on the bonfires, but it is not indignation over the Plot which has ensured the survival of this now-traditional custom, but rather the instinctive attraction which a bonfire holds for us all, young and old alike. In Sheffield, where six public bonfires have been burned annually in the major parks since 1969, it was found that in 1981 a minimum of 60,000 people attended the public bonfires, that is one in eight of Sheffield residents; and many others attended smaller local bonfires.

Helston Furry Dance, Cornwall

Date: 8 May
Location: Helston is 9 miles south-west of Falmouth.

The date of this event is the Feast of the Apparition of St Michael Archangel, the town's patron saint. Its origins are however pre-Christian, and the dance is a survival of the great spring festivals celebrating the continuance of life. The song sung early in the morning by the youngsters who fetch green branches and then parade the streets, shows what the event signifies:

> With Hal-an-Tow! Jolly Rumble, O!
> For we are up as soon as any day, O,
> And for to fetch the Summer home,
> The Summer and the May, O.
> For Summer is a-come, O,
> And Winter is a-gone, O.

The first dance begins at 7 o'clock and is danced by young people. This is followed by the children's dance, and then at noon the Chief Dance, led by the Mayor. The couples dance around the town, bringing the luck of summer to all whose homes they enter. The dances continue until late afternoon, by which time everyone is taking part and the town is filled with dancers.

Flambeaux Procession, Comrie, Perthshire/Tayside Region

Date: 31 December
Location: Comrie is 18 miles north of Stirling.

On New Year's Eve the townspeople gather in the square at midnight, when a procession of men in costume and carrying huge torches begins to wend its way around the town and then back to the square, led by pipes and followed by the crowd. The flambeaux are then piled on the ground to make a bonfire, and everyone dances until the flames have died down, thus burning out the old year and welcoming the new.

231

Minehead Hobby Horse Festival, Somerset

Date: 1 May
Location: Minehead is in north-west Somerset, on the coast.

Minehead Hobby Horse as he appeared on 1 May 1925.

Although the Minehead horse is as ancient as Padstow's, he is very different in appearance, with his ringed body and a long

232

mane of streamers. He used to have a horse's head with snapping jaws, but the head of the man inside the framework is now covered by a high, pointed cap and a ferocious mask. This 'Sailors' Horse' tours the towns of Minehead and Dunster from early morning, and until recently was accompanied by two Gullivers, men who used 'persuasion' to extract donations from people. As at other rituals of early spring, such as Padstow and the Helston Furry Dance, the intention is to draw in good luck to the people and their houses. People are glad to have the Minehead horse dance outside their houses, or even inside, for he is bestowing good luck upon them for the year.

Arbor Day, Aston-on-Clun, Shropshire

Date: 29 May, or thereabouts
Location: Aston-on-Clun is 9 miles north-west of Ludlow.

The central event in the festivities at Aston-on-Clun is the dressing of a black poplar tree in the centre of the village with flags, though on the day itself only the flag of St George is ceremonially raised. This custom is said to celebrate a wedding which took place two hundred years ago, but is more likely to be the remnants of ancient tree worship, which was once widespread. Now the ceremony is somewhat prettified, with the children in costume re-enacting the wedding procession and dancing round a miniature maypole, but Morris dancers who bring a more boisterous atmosphere also perform and the ceremony is followed by a village fête and amusements.

Abbots Bromley Horn Dance, Staffordshire

Date: In September, the Monday following the first Sunday after the 4th.
Location: Abbots Bromley is 9 miles east of Stafford.

Another thriving custom with exceedingly ancient origins is the Horn Dance, now performed in September in the local wakes week but originally a winter solstice ritual, being performed at Christmas, on New Year's Day, and at Twelfth Night. Six men carrying reindeer antlers are accompanied by the Fool, Maid Marian (a man dressed as a woman; for more discussion of the fascinating 'she-male' see our earlier book *Earth Rites*), a Hobby Horse, a Bowman, a boy with a triangle, and a musician. Throughout the day the dancers perform their simple spiral

233

Abbots Bromley Horn Dancers (note Maid Marian and the Hobby Horse together on the left) in action in 1979.

dance at traditional points in a circle of over 20 miles around the parish, finally returning to the village to dance in the centre before returning the antlers to the church where they are kept from year to year.

Sword dancing, in northern England

Date: Usually in winter.

Sword dances were once performed as part of folk plays, and originally came to northern England from Denmark. They are part of the rites of winter, with the death of the old year and the birth of the new, depicted in the plays by the beheading by the sword dancers of a victim who then returned to life. The decapitation takes place when all the swords are locked together in a 'lock' or 'glass'; sometimes the swords when locked are held up to represent the sun.

Sword dancers can still be seen at Grenoside and Handsworth, both in Sheffield (South Yorkshire) on Boxing Day; Ripon (North Yorkshire) in the Sword Dance Play on Boxing Day; Greatham (Cleveland) on Boxing Day; and Goathland (North Yorkshire) as part of the Plough Stots early in January.

234

19. *Aligning ancient sites: earth energy paths*

Archaeological investigation is usually aimed at preserving as much evidence as possible of the lives of ancient peoples, both structures and artefacts. Archaeologists concern themselves with minutiae to the ultimate degree, and are so skilled that they can 'read' soil layers and fragments of pottery to gradually build up the past history of a site. Experience, instinct and expectation combine to present a cohesive picture of a people and their life-style; but archaeologists are also human and therefore not infallible, and the degree of expectation involved can affect their interpretation of the evidence, so that it often tells them what they expect to be told. As they are dealing with the relics of civilisations as much as 12,000 years old, and are acknowledged as the 'experts', it is difficult for any outsider to effectively challenge their pronouncements, but it is interesting to look back and see how on occasion the certainties of one archaeological generation have been reversed by the next, thus proving that archaeologists are less certain of the accuracy of their interpretations than they would have the general public believe. This is not to belittle their skills in locating and preserving the buried evidence, merely to suggest that their interpretations of that evidence should not necessarily be accepted uncritically.

During the past twenty years some alternative views of the past have been offered which credit our prehistoric ancestors with skills which we ourselves have long since lost. In this new view they are portrayed not as savages wresting a meagre living from an unfriendly environment, but as Stone Age technicians who had an innate sensitivity which enabled them to be aware of the flow of the earth's natural energies and to manipulate these energies to their benefit. However, the proponents of such theories fall into the same trap as the archaeologists, in that their theories also tend to be coloured by their hopes and expectations, and again it is exceedingly difficult to judge which theories are based on reliable evidence and which on wish-fulfilling pseudo-evidence. There is hardly room in this short chapter to do justice to all the ideas which have been aired in the past twenty years, but we will outline the major ones, and we suggest that readers eager to learn more should obtain the relevant books listed in the Bibliography.

The most widely known unorthodox theory is that ancient sites sometimes align, a theory originally propounded by Alfred Watkins (1855–1935) of Hereford. He called the alignments he found 'leys' (now widely but incorrectly called 'ley-lines'), and first published his researches in 1925 in *The Old Straight Track*. In brief a ley is defined as an alignment of ancient sites, such as hillforts, stone circles, standing stones, burial chambers and tumuli, churches on old sites, and other sites with ancient origins such as trackways, moats, crossroads, holy wells. Watkins saw the alignments as ancient trackways, often sighted on natural horizon features such as peaks and notches, and he often found evidence of long-hidden trackways along the course of his leys. Interestingly, in recent years a similar system of straight

Wearyall Hill photographed from Glastonbury Tor (Somerset). Britain's mystical centre of Glastonbury has already featured several times in this book. In this chapter we describe the Glastonbury Zodiac (see 'Places to Visit'), in which Wearyall Hill forms one of the two fishes in the Pisces figure. A seven-point ley 21 miles long also passes through Glastonbury Tor (for details see Paul Devereux and Ian Thomson's Ley Hunter's Companion*).*

paths has been discovered in Peru. For example, from the Coricancha or Sun Temple in the centre of the city of Cuzco, forty-one lines called *ceques* radiated out across the countryside, their routes marked by *huacas* or holy shrines in the form of springs, hills, caves, bridges, houses, battlefields and tombs. Some of the *ceques* were also astronomical sight lines, which is one interpretation which has recently been applied to some leys in Britain.

Watkins's ley theory languished in obscurity for many years, until it was rediscovered and *The Old Straight Track* republished in 1970. It was followed in the 1970s by a new generation of books on leys, taking the theory further and introducing mystical aspects. The most notable books of this period were John Michell's *The View Over Atlantis* (now reissued as *The New View Over Atlantis*), Paul Screeton's *Quicksilver Heritage* and Paul Devereux and Ian Thomson's *The Ley Hunter's Companion.* Researchers into all aspects of leys have been served for twenty years by a lively magazine, *The Ley Hunter* (The Coach House, Mount Street, Brecon, Powys), in which the latest theories are aired, research is published, and controversy flourishes. For controversy is never absent in the world of leys, the major controversy for years having centred on the basic questions: Do the purported alignments really exist, and if so, are they due to chance or do they have some major significance? Researchers are still working to find conclusive answers to these questions, and we do not have the space here to even summarise the many thousands of words which have already been written.

Continuing with the assumption that leys do exist and are not just due to chance, we can briefly outline a few intriguing aspects of the research at present being conducted. Many researchers believe that leys mark the course of a subtle 'earth energy' whose nature is unclear but may be related to terrestrial magnetism. The construction of earthworks such as burial mounds, and possibly also some so-called hillforts, may have been part of a scheme of landscape engineering designed to enhance and direct the natural earth energies which were then channelled along leys in order to bring greater fertility and well-being to all life on the planet. Stone circles and standing stones may also have had a part to play, the standing stones possibly being used as stone needles to earth the current. It has been noticed that quartz stones have often been used (for example at Boscawen-Un, see Chapter 1), and quartz has many interesting qualities apart from its visual attractiveness. It can produce an electric current when put under tension or pressure,

237

and when it is influenced by an electric field it will vibrate rapidly at frequencies measured in millions per second and is therefore used in resonators and oscillators for frequency control in electronic communications equipment. Granite usually contains between 20 and 40 per cent quartz, and many standing stones and circles must contain a large amount of this substance. Many examples of its use are given in our earlier book *The Secret Country*.

Some people can sense what may be energy currents when touching standing stones, as did one of our correspondents during a visit with her family to the circles at Stanton Drew (Avon) in 1981:

> Having negotiated half of the first circle, mostly discussing the actual geology of the stones with the boys, we both experimentally and half-jokingly placed both hands on a stone and shut our eyes. Even with the boys chattering and asking questions, we both received differing sensations. He felt a tingling sensation in his fingers and had the sensation that the stone was moving, as if it was floating upwards. Being sceptical, his mind rejected the feeling and he said nothing at first. Meanwhile I was keeping quiet about what I had felt. When my hands were on the stone I could feel my body moving from the hips in an oval movement anticlockwise. I was a little shaken and it was not until I asked if he had felt anything too that my companion described what he had felt . . . At the last stone, which we had only examined geologically as we came in, we had a final experiment. I found a very strong force pushing me to the left and my friend felt the same tingling and lightness but this time accompanied by a feeling almost of evil which he did not like, a different sensation from the other stones.

On another occasion she experienced a tingling sensation when touching the Harold's Stones at Trellech (Gwent): 'On the largest stone I felt the same movements, an anticlockwise wide oval, but gradually changing into a small circle going smaller and faster until it faded and went back to the larger oval pattern again and repeated.' She remarked that at both Stanton Drew and the Harold's Stones there is quartz visible in the stones, especially the largest stone at Trellech, and it is possible that the quartz was in some way responsible for the sensations she experienced.

Another approach to the search for earth energies is through dowsing. This is a versatile skill not used solely for the discovery of underground water sources, but adaptable to the search for anything from corpses to subtle energy currents. In his book *Needles of Stone* Tom Graves demonstrates the wide-ranging use of dowsing in this field of exploration. Dowsing is just one

A Dragon Project experiment at the Rollright Stones in 1979, involving dowsing, biofeedback and a mind mirror. Among the participants are Maxwell Cade (left) with dowsing rods, Tom Graves (centre) and Geoff Blundell.

of the many techniques employed in the Dragon Project, a programme of monitoring the prehistoric structures at Rollright in Oxfordshire which began in 1978. Other techniques used include ultrasonic detection, microwave monitoring, electric field detection, geiger monitoring, experimental infra-red photography, and clairvoyance. The Dragon Project involves scientists and physicists, and is an indication of how the two opposite poles are gradually coming together. After many years of mutual disapproval, archaeologists and ley-researchers arc now also beginning to work together, and all the signs are that earth energies research is sct to lose its 'lunatic fringe' image.

Apart from the nature of the rock from which standing stones are fashioned, their shape also seems to have had some significance. We have already illustrated some variations in shape – alternating diamond and pillar stones in the Kennet Avenue, stones like the Devil's Arrows which Tom Graves likens to needles or nails driven into the ground, and stones which echo the shapes of hills close by, a good example being the stone at Kinnerton (all these stones described in Chapter 4). These shapes were chosen for some important reasons which are not understood today, but if earth energies can be controlled by the judicious use of shaped standing stones, then the specific shapes may have played an important role, perhaps to maximise the efficient channelling of the energy. People who have experimented with pyramid-shapes have found them to be active as energy collectors, but with unexpected effects: one researcher's quartz-controlled digital watch became erratic and finally stopped altogether, much to the surprise of the manufacturers. The similarity between the pyramid shape and the standing stone shape is close, and also very similar is the church spire. We have already described the siting of churches at prehistoric sites and their close connection with holy wells. Dowsers exploring churches have sometimes found the church plan conforming to the configuration of underground water sources, and there is other evidence that the church builders of past centuries were following ancient practices designed to enhance the spiritual energy within the structure.

Earth mysteries researchers working in this new field during the past twenty years have found many tantalising hints concerning the nature of earth energies and their use by people in ages past. Much more research remains to be done, however, and some of the lines of research being followed will inevitably turn out to be blind alleys. But there can be no doubt that there is fire to be found among the clouds of smoke, and that Alfred Watkins started an important new line of research when he began to follow the leys in the rural byways of his native Herefordshire over sixty years ago.

PLACES TO VISIT

Old Sarum ley, Wiltshire and Hampshire

Location: Old Sarum – SU 1332

This alignment runs for 18½ miles and passes through six sites: a tumulus, Stonehenge, Old Sarum, Salisbury Cathedral, Clearbury Ring hillfort, Frankenbury Camp hillfort. The photograph shows three of the sites – Old Sarum in the foreground, then the spire of Salisbury Cathedral aligning with the edge of the earthworks of Clearbury Ring. The ley passes just along the outer banks of both hillforts, a feature noticed by Alfred Watkins and common in leys passing through hillforts.

Old Sarum is an intriguing site, having begun as an Iron Age fort, of which a deep outer ditch remains. Inside a settlement grew up in Roman times, which was later occupied by the Saxons, and then a Norman castle was built, the considerable ruins of which can still be seen. In the eleventh century a cathedral was founded here, but two hundred years later the

Old Sarum ley.

site was abandoned and a new cathedral founded in the nearby water meadows, where Salisbury Cathedral still stands. The foundations and chapter house crypt of the old cathedral survive and can be visited.

The alignment of Stonehenge with Old Sarum, Salisbury Cathedral and Clearbury Ring was first noticed by Sir Norman Lockyer, an archaeologist working at the beginning of this century who also noticed other alignments of ancient sites and believed that they indicated sunrise and sunset at certain times of the year. This alignment was checked and extended by Paul Devereux and Ian Thomson for publication in their classic ley-hunting work, *The Ley Hunter's Companion.*

Montgomery ley.

Montgomery ley, Powys and Shropshire

Location: Montgomery – SO 2296

This Welsh border ley covers nearly 6 miles and takes in six sites: Offa's Dyke crossed by a lane at a high point with an extensive view for several miles as far as Montgomery town; half a mile of straight road along the line of the ley; Montgomery church; Montgomery Castle on a high point; Hendomen, the motte and bailey castle predating the Norman castle and present town of Montgomery; Forden Gaer, a Roman camp by an ancient ford across the River Severn.

Standing on the extensive castle ruins, you can look back towards the church and see beyond it (in winter when the trees are bare) the length of aligning road. This ley was discovered by Paul Devereux, editor of *The Ley Hunter*, who saw the church and castle aligning with the road he was following into Montgomery.

242

Llanthony Priory ley, Gwent

Location: Llanthony Priory – SO 289278

> In the deep vale of Ewias ... encircled on all sides by lofty mountains, stands the church ... Here the monks, sitting in their cloisters, enjoying the fresh air, when they happen to look up towards the horizon, behold the tops of the mountains as it were touching the heavens, and herds of wild deer feeding on their summits.

This is Giraldus Cambrensis' description of Llanthony Priory in the twelfth century, and although the priory is now ruined and the monks no longer there, this is still a beautiful place, tucked away on the eastern edge of the Black Mountains where Powys, Gwent and Herefordshire come together.

The short four-point ley at Llanthony was noted by Alfred Watkins, who described and illustrated it in his *Old Straight Track*:

> A short length of hollow, grassy roadway sights up to a sharp notch on the northern ridge. Planting sighting rods for this alignment, and then sighting backward ... the ley passes through the chancel of the original priory (for this is the second building), and then falls upon one of the three deep gullies or tracks which steeply climb the central ridge. It is a good four-point example – the notch, the fragment of old road in the valley, the church on the ley, the steep track up the mountain.

The photograph shows the priory and the steep tracks up the ridge beyond; behind us are the old road and the notch.

Llanthony Priory ley.

Glastonbury Zodiac, Somerset

Glastonbury is famous for its Arthurian connections (see Chapter 14) and as a mystical centre, and the two are linked in another mystery which extends over a 10-mile wide circle south of Glastonbury, the so-called Glastonbury Zodiac. This was discovered in the 1920s by Katherine Maltwood, who plotted the quest of King Arthur's Knights in search of the Holy Grail on to maps and decided that she had discovered the Round Table in the form of a zodiac. The outlines of the figures are formed by natural features such as roads and tracks, field and woodland boundaries, rivers and streams. Glastonbury itself is covered by the Aquarius figure, here depicted as a phoenix, the mythical bird which rose from the fire. The Tor falls within the

Ponter's Ball.

head of the bird, Chalice Hill forms its body; in Chalice Well some believe the Holy Grail to lie. Close by is Wearyall Hill, which in the zodiac forms one of the two fishes in the figure of Pisces. According to the legend, it was on Wearyall Hill that Joseph of Arimathea stuck his staff into the ground, from which grew the Holy Thorn of Glastonbury. (Wearyall Hill was illustrated earlier in this chapter.) Ponter's Ball, illustrated here, is an earthwork not far from Glastonbury which forms the horn of the goat, the Capricorn figure.

In the fifty or sixty years since Katherine Maltwood's discovery of the zodiac its details have been refined by Mary Caine and others, and researchers whose imaginations have been fired by the zodiac have pored over maps and discovered their own zodiacs, but without the Arthurian connections, in other parts of the country. However, the very ubiquity of the zodiacs tends to cast doubt on their reality. There are so many features on any Ordnance Survey map that the chances are you could find the outlines of a zodiac just about anywhere, if you looked hard enough and were prepared to bend the rules when necessary (as has happened, even in the original Glastonbury zodiac). Do terrestrial zodiacs really exist, or are they simply 'pictures in the fire'?

20. *Modern mysteries*

Lest we have given the impression in the previous nineteen chapters that the mysteries in Britain are all ancient, we will close our tour with some twentieth-century mysteries, all of them still unsolved and many of them still taking place. Strange phenomena of this kind are regularly reported in a unique publication which has now been providing its readers with the latest news on modern mysteries for ten years – *Fortean Times* (96 Mansfield Road, London NW3 2HX), which is edited by the leading researcher and writer in this field, Robert J. M. Rickard (see Bibliography for details of his books), and his colleague Paul Sieveking. Mysteries of the kind we describe in this chapter are now receiving more attention than hitherto. Apart from *Fortean Times*, and our own books *Alien Animals* and *Modern British Mysteries* (the latter in preparation), a new series of paperback books on mysteries which began publication in 1983 has received praise for its high standard of authorship and responsible attitude towards its subject matter. In 'The Evidence for ...' series (Thorsons Publishers), the titles currently available are *UFOs, Visions of the Virgin Mary, Alien Abductions, Bigfoot and Other Man-Beasts, Phantom Hitch-Hikers,* and *The Bermuda Triangle*, with others in preparation.

The Evidence for UFOs was chosen as the title to begin the series, and not surprisingly, for UFOs are a truly modern mystery, and perhaps one of the greatest. They came into prominence in the late 1940s, but during the subsequent forty years they have prompted massive media coverage and have become a worldwide phenomenon of extraordinary variety and baffling complexity. Britain has had its fair share of UFO mysteries, ranging from the 'flying crosses' of the late 1960s through the Warminster hysteria of the 1970s (see 'Places to Visit') to the 'alien landing' at a US Air Force base in Rendlesham Forest, East Anglia, in 1980 (see Butler, Street and Randles, *Sky Crash*, for the full story).

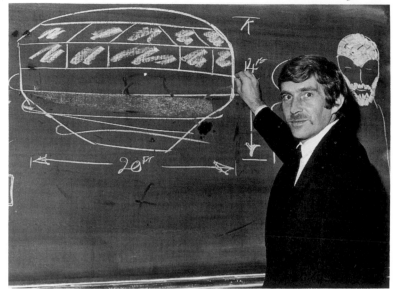

PC Alan Godfrey draws the UFO into which he was abducted in November 1980 from his patrol car in Todmorden, West Yorkshire. (The full story and details of the interviews under hypnosis will be found in Jenny Randles's book The Pennine UFO Mystery.*)*

UFOs have never attracted properly funded scientific attention, but fortunately a number of scientists have been sufficiently intrigued to voluntarily devote themselves to the problem. Although there is still no definitive answer to the question 'What are UFOs?', ufology has come a long way since the first sightings of what, in the late 1940s, were called 'flying saucers' and it is now possible to separate the so-called UFOs into two categories – IFOs (identifiable flying objects) and 'true UFOs' (a new type of phenomenon). In the former category the major stimuli which cause people to sincerely believe they are seeing something inexplicable are rare natural phenomena like ball lightning and common natural phenomena like the moon, which is misidentified surprisingly often, though it can look very strange under certain conditions, such as when veiled in cloud. Researchers have found that not only are many people unfamiliar with the night sky, but they have been conditioned by media coverage to call any inexplicable sighting a 'UFO' without looking very hard for a natural explanation. This conditioning is usually unconscious in that they are unaware of the extent of their knowledge of UFO lore, until it surfaces in the form of a purported UFO experience, sometimes of a very weird nature, which eventually turns out to be a fantasy triggered when in a dissociated state by a slightly unusual stimulus, such as an unfamiliar planet seen in the night sky while the witness is driving, a state now known to be conducive to at least partial dissociation.

However, not all UFO events can yet be explained in this way. There is no space here to give specific examples, but plenty will be found in the relevant books in the Bibliography (authors to look for are Randles and Evans). The hypothesis that UFOs are the space vehicles of beings from Mars, or any other planet, in or outside our galaxy, has been largely discounted by serious ufologists, though this explanation is still widely accepted by uncritical UFO enthusiasts, especially in the USA. Whether UFOs are craft of any kind, and whether they contain entities, are still unanswered questions despite forty years devoted to trying to answer them.

Ghosts and poltergeists are mysteries which have been studied for far longer, but like UFOs remain unexplained. They are perennial mysteries in that new cases come to light year after year, but little scientific work is being done to track down the mechanism which causes ghosts and poltergeists to manifest. At first glance it might seem strange that science is so unenthusiastic about tackling such obvious and proven mysteries as UFOs and ghosts, but these phenomena cannot be produced on demand or studied in the laboratory, and researchers usually find themselves with nothing more substantial to work on than witness reports. This secondhand level of investigation, coupled with the ridicule generally directed at such subjects, ensures that scientists have to be really keen, and not too concerned about promotion, before they will involve themselves with such chimerical phenomena.

The same attitude is taken by scientists faced with reports of monsters or unexpected animals, which are regularly seen throughout Britain, be they lake monsters of the Nessie variety, or big cats roaming the wilds of darkest Surrey. The scientists demand a corpse before they will begin to show an interest, witness reports and even photographs being notoriously unreliable, since the camera *can* appear to lie in that a skilful photographer can produce hoax photographs only identifiable as such after skilled and detailed examination, and maybe not even then. The Loch Ness Monster is probably the best-known lake monster in the world, but even though she first became headline news over fifty years ago, there is still no solid proof of her, or rather their, existence in the lake, and only a handful of photographs exist, most of them dubious in one way or another (the best photograph obtained so far is shown in 'Places to Visit'). Many other lakes in Scotland, Wales and Ireland are also said to be the homes of lake monsters, but serious investigation is expensive and is hampered by the nature of the creature's

248

environment. Although many sightings can be explained away as waves, sticks and birds, seen at a distance by excited witnesses, there are others which are less easy to explain, where a strange creature was seen at close quarters, as happened to Alphonsus Mullaney and his father, of the same name, in March 1962. Alphonsus Mullaney senior was a teacher in Glinsk, and the encounter took place at Lough Dubh near Glinsk (County Galway). Mr Mullaney described what happened to a *Sunday Review* reporter:

> We were working on the bog after school and I had promised to take young Alphonsus fishing. We carried a twelve foot rod with a strong line and spoon bait for perch or pike, of which there are plenty in Lough Dubh.
>
> For a while I let the boy fish with the rod and used a shorter rod with worm bait, but I got no 'answer'. After five minutes I decided that the fish were not there that evening, but I took the long rod and walked up and down the bank.
>
> Suddenly there was a tugging on the line. I thought it might be caught on a root, so I took it gently. It did not give. I hauled it slowly ashore, and the line snapped. I was examining the line when the lad screamed.
>
> Then I saw the animal. It was not a seal or anything I had ever seen. It had for instance short thick legs, and a hippo face. It was as big as a cow or an ass, square faced, with small ears and a white pointed horn on its snout. It was dark grey in colour, and covered with bristles or short hair, like a pig.

The creature was apparently enraged by the pain after trying to take the baited hook, and also annoyed by a barking dog, and tried to climb out of the water to attack the boy, who screamed and ran to his father. They both hurried away, and informed local people of their sighting, so that armed men soon converged on the lake, but nothing was seen. Later Alphonsus junior identified a rhinoceros in a picture book of animals as being closest to what he had seen.

As this strange report indicates, the lake monsters do not all conform to the same description – most lake monsters do not look like rhinoceroses, but have long necks and small heads. It is likely that there are several different types of unknown creature lurking in our lakes. Recent expeditions into unexplored country in the heart of Africa have produced convincing reports, and a sighting by a scientist, of a large and hitherto unknown lake creature believed to be a type of dinosaur. If this can happen in Africa, why not in Britain, where there are also large areas of unpopulated and relatively unexplored terrain with deep and remote lakes where all kinds of unknown creatures could have lived undisturbed for millions of years. This is one mystery which may be explained eventually, and so too may the mystery of the British big cat. For many years, but especially during the last twenty years, reports have been made by apparently sane citizens of big cats seen lurking in the undergrowth – usually described as pumas or panthers (the same animal, also known as the mountain lion), but occasionally other species are named such as the lion or cheetah. These reports do not appear in isolation, but in waves. The so-called 'Surrey puma' is perhaps the best-known example, with hundreds of reports received by police during the early 1960s from rural Surrey and adjoining Hampshire, and sporadic reports continue to be made from this area. There is hardly an area of mainland Britain (also the Isle of Wight!) from which reports have not come, but in recent years they have most often come from Exmoor (Somerset/Devon border), the Inverness area, and Caithness; also Ayrshire, Nottinghamshire, Cheshire, Berkshire, Buckinghamshire, Norfolk, Lincolnshire, Sussex, Kent, Devon, Powys, Dyfed and Glamorgan.

The evidence that big cats are living wild in Britain is now overwhelming, yet still not officially accepted – perhaps because it is feared that people would panic if they were told that big cats are on the loose in large numbers. However, these cats generally avoid human habitations and certainly will not attack humans unless provoked. The reason why they are being seen more often now is in part likely to be due to the fact that there are less wilderness areas for them to inhabit, as humans steadily encroach into the untouched countryside. They may also come close to settlements in search of food, especially if they are breeding successfully and thus increasing their numbers. They are thought to live mainly on wild creatures such as rabbits, though sheep are sometimes killed in a manner suggestive of cats, and on such occasions the creatures get wide publicity, especially if sighted, as happened in the early 1980s on Exmoor when many savage attacks on sheep and lambs were suffered, behaviour untypical of the British big cat.

As with any alien creature, the Establishment demands a corpse before it will take the reports seriously. The big cats are too cautious to be easily killed or trapped (on Exmoor armed Marines specially called in were unsuccessful) but it has happened. There have been several reports over the decades of huntsmen and farmers killing unidentifiable animals, but they always disposed of the corpse and the killing has only become known to researchers years later. In 1980 a farmer at Cannich

250

near Inverness actually managed to trap a fully grown female puma in a cage, but experts stated that the cat was tame and had never lived in the wild! Four years later the stuffed body of a black cat shot in Morayshire in 1982 was examined by scientists at the Natural History Museum in London and identified as a Scottish wild cat, not a puma, but they were baffled because of its colour – wild cats are tabby, definitely not black. They decided it must be a rare melanistic (black) mutation. Interestingly, black pumas are now frequently reported in the States, although pumas are not usually black and naturalists declare that black ones are very rare. There are known to be other black wild cats breeding in the area of Scotland where this cat and two others were shot. This melanistic wild cat does not however explain the many sightings of non-black cats in areas where wild cats are not native, such as Surrey, and the big cats reported are much bigger than wild cats. The search for an answer, and preferably further corpses, will continue, headed by naturalist Di Francis whose book *Cat Country* describes many intriguing encounters with these UFOs – unidentified furry objects. We also wrote about the big cats, along with lake monsters, in our earlier book *Alien Animals*.

UFOs, ghosts and alien animals are not the only mysteries

A comparison between a plaster cast of a zoo puma's paw print (right) and one of the prints of the Munstead Monster, found near Godalming (Surrey) on 7 September 1964.

still occurring in Britain today. In our next book, *Modern British Mysteries*, we shall also describe sightings of ball lightning and phantom black dogs, mysterious deaths and disappearances, falls of fishes, frogs, ice and other unexpected objects from the sky, unidentified humming noises, phantom armies, out-of-place animals such as porcupines, raccoons, wallabies, crocodiles and boars, spontaneous human combustion, teleportation, toads and frogs embedded in rocks, and many other strange phenomena reliably reported in the twentieth century in Britain.

PLACES TO VISIT

Borley Rectory, Essex

Location: In the hamlet of Borley, 2 miles north-west of Sudbury on the Essex/Suffolk border. (TL 847430)

'The most haunted house in England' no longer exists, having been burnt down in 1939 and the ruin later demolished. Whether the old rectory ever deserved that title bestowed upon it by ghost-hunter Harry Price is now open to doubt. The events which reportedly took place there engendered thousands of words, including several books, and at this late date the truth can probably never be known, but it has been suggested that a large part of the phenomena consisted of hoaxes, by more than one person, and that most of the rest was the result of poor eyesight or simple misidentification of natural events, by people keyed up in expectation of ghosts.

Borley church, just across the road, is also said to be haunted. Singing and chanting and organ music have been heard from the locked church, objects inside were moved overnight, again in the locked church, footsteps and other strange noises have been heard, and the ringing of the church bell, though the church was again locked. In 1949 a visiting priest saw the figure of a veiled girl who moved behind shrubs and was nowhere to be seen when the priest went to investigate. He said that she looked frail, and 'had the shape of a nun's hood on her head from which hung the thick veiling – her features were not discernible.' Other ghostly figures have been seen in the churchyard, including in 1967 a 'luminous white figure' which changed into a luminous white patch. This so alarmed the four witnesses that

they decided to leave – only to find that their car unexpectedly refused to start. On other occasions the close presence of other strange phenomena such as UFOs and alien animals has had this same effect on cars.

The road separating Borley church from the site of Borley Rectory, which is behind the trees on our left.

Many ghost-hunters who have visited this area over the last fifty years have reported strange phenomena of some kind, either around the site of the rectory, by the adjacent cottage, in the road outside, or around the church. There is some evidence to suggest that at least some phenomena are created involuntarily by the witnesses, and it seems likely that the people who visit Borley in a state of tension and excitement are prime candidates for subconsciously creating ghostly phenomena (through a mechanism not yet understood) which they then report as objective happenings. On the other hand, of course, there just might be evil spirits lurking around the scene of ancient crimes, appreciating the attention bestowed upon them by easily frightened 'ghost-hunters'!

253

Hampton Court Palace, Greater London

Location: Beside the River Thames, 2 miles south-west of Kingston-upon-Thames. (TQ 1568)

Judging by the number of ghosts reportedly seen there, Hampton Court Palace must be one of the most haunted places in England, and much more deserving of the title than Borley Rectory. The ghosts include several of King Henry VIII's wives. Jane Seymour is said to walk through Clock Court and the Silver Stick Gallery, carrying a lighted taper; Anne Boleyn has also been seen; but the best-known apparition is that of his fifth wife, Catherine Howard, who was arrested in 1541 only a year after her marriage on a charge of adultery. At the time of her arrest the King was in the chapel nearby, and she escaped from her guards and ran to plead for his mercy, shrieking frantically. But he ignored her cries and she was dragged away. Now she is sometimes seen running screaming through what is now known as the Haunted Gallery.

Unidentified ghosts have been seen in the grounds, like the group of eight or nine ladies and two men in evening dress, seen by a policeman in Ditton Walk. They vanished as he watched them. Actor Leslie French saw a figure in Tudor costume whom he thought must be one of the actresses from a performance of *Twelfth Night*, but she was not seen by Lady Grant who was accompanying him, though she did feel a coldness in the air as Mr French moved aside to let the ghost pass.

As Hampton Court Palace is a very popular tourist attraction, it is best visited out of season if you wish to try and sense the haunted atmosphere. Would any self-respecting ghost put in an appearance among crowds of tourists? Perhaps it would, for ghosts usually look as solid as living people, and unless they do something unexpected like walking through a wall or vanishing in mid-air, you are unlikely to realise that you are seeing a ghost and not a living person. So a ghost could easily blend in unnoticed among a tourist crowd (though it might appear to be wearing theatrical costume!), and might appreciate the opportunity to wander unrecognised around former haunts.

Warminster, Wiltshire

Location: 6 miles south-east of Frome; Cradle Hill is approached along a lane leading to the hill from the south-west. (Cradle Hill – ST 886467)

Twenty years ago in 1965, Warminster was gripped by a UFO-fever which developed into a mania for standing on Cradle Hill and watching the night sky in the hope of seeing 'something' – this madness not affecting the bulk of the local residents, we hasten to add, but principally visitors from all corners of the United Kingdom and overseas too. It all began when UFOs seen in the area were investigated and reported in the local press by Arthur Shuttlewood, a local journalist who soon fell under the spell of 'the Thing'. He began to write a series of books with titles like *Warnings from Flying Friends* and *UFO Magic in Motion*, and spent many hours sky-watching on Cradle Hill, accompanied by crowds of fans who supported his philosophy. Many lights were seen from Cradle Hill, but there is little doubt that most of them had straightforward explanations. With the presence of the army on the hills close by, flares and other military activity could account for many 'UFOs', while one of us on a visit to a Cradle Hill sky-watch in the late 1960s, watching an obvious satellite passing overhead, heard it described enthusiastically as a UFO. Hoaxes were also perpetrated, successfully fooling many people, and by the late 1970s this UFO-Mecca became discredited. Cradle Hill now stands silent on Saturday nights, except perhaps for a few pilgrims reliving the thrilling nights of their innocent youth.

Llyn Tegid/Bala Lake, Gwynedd

Location: South-west of Bala town, and 15 miles north-east of Dolgellau.

Scotland and Ireland both have many lakes reputedly the home of a lake monster or two, but the Welsh lakes of both mountain and lowland are apparently lacking in those denizens of the deep. The exception is Llyn Tegid, a picturesque stretch of water much used for water sports, under the surface of which is said to be submerged the original town of Bala, overwhelmed as a punishment. Several people have reported seeing a large unidentifiable creature in the water during the last twenty years, including Bala greengrocer John Rowlands, who with his cousin saw something strange when fishing in the lake some time during the 1970s. He said:

> We were fishing on the bank in dead calm water. All of a sudden, the thing reared up and started heading towards us. It had a large head like a football and rather big eyes. We could see the body which was

Bala Lake.

nearly 8 feet long. It wasn't aggressive at all. It swam towards us to within a few yards and then turned and disappeared. I wouldn't say I had seen a monster, it was just a large being. But I have caught some rather big pike in the lake before now and it was bigger than any of those.

He also came up with a possible explanation. 'During the first world war they used to use live seals in the lake for submarine detection training. I don't know the lifespan of a seal, but that is the only thing the creature resembles. Its skin had a black shiny surface.' However, if seals were in the lake, they would surely be seen more often. Lake warden Dewi Bowen had seen the creature and also knew of other sightings: 'I saw it once and it looked a bit like a crocodile ... Then two other fishermen in a boat saw something breaking the surface. It scared the living daylights out of them.'

One of two photographs of the Loch Ness Monster taken by Anthony Shiels on 21 May 1977 from Urquhart Castle. He was less than 100 yards from the creature, the visible part of whose neck appeared to be 4 or 5 feet long. It was in sight only for a few seconds before sinking smoothly below the surface.

Loch Ness, Inverness/Highland Region

Location: South-west of Inverness.

Loch Ness is nearly 25 miles long, a mile wide and in places as much as 900 feet deep, and it is therefore hardly surprising that

256

the various expeditions mounted during the past twenty-five years have obtained no definite proof of the existence of large and unknown animals living in the loch. A lack of finance inevitably restricts the scope of the investigations, and despite their valiant efforts, which have become ever more scientific since the early days of camera surveillance, there are no corpses, not even any bones, nor any flesh samples; of the few photographs that exist, none is sharp or detailed and most are of doubtful authenticity; and the many misidentifications and undoubted hoaxes have been seized upon by the sceptics to support their anti-Nessie arguments. All of which is very frustrating for those who have actually seen the creature and know that it is something unknown to science.

Although most witnesses have seen the monster, or something which they thought might be the monster, when it was in the water, there are a few who have seen it on land, and these are potentially the most informative reports since the whole body can be seen. There are twelve or thirteen such reports covering the years 1879–1960. Most witnesses saw a large creature with a greyish body, a long neck and small head, moving with a waddling motion on short thick legs or flippers. The creature was usually seen on the shore, but once or twice it crossed the road in front of the startled witnesses. This apparent ability to exist on land as well as in the water could explain why small Irish loughs where monsters have been seen proved to be empty when netted (see for example Lough Nahooin described elsewhere in 'Places to Visit'). The creatures may even wander about from loch to loch, especially in Ireland where in some areas the lakes are close together and in unpopulated country. Perhaps the investigators' attention should be switched to the smaller Irish loughs where recent sightings have occurred. Then if the existence of previously unknown creatures in Irish loughs can be proved, finance might be more readily available to assist the search in Loch Ness.

Napton on the Hill church, Warwickshire

Location: Napton is 9 miles south-west of Rugby. (SP 463612)

The church is said to have been built on the hilltop at the wish of the fairies or earth spirits, who every night moved uphill the stones which were being erected down below. The church was also said to be connected to the former vicarage, now demolished, by a secret passage; and it was also believed that to run three times round the church at night would raise the Devil. Most definitely a supernatural place!

Several people have seen ghosts in and around the church, which has been haunted for several hundred years. In 1820 the Reverend Augustus Fent was temporarily in charge of the church, and returning there one evening he saw two women in grey cloaks kneeling in the front pew. Wondering how they had entered the locked church, he shone his lantern on them, whereupon they disappeared. He had not heard about these ghosts of two Elizabethan ladies who were often seen over several generations. More recently, two boys walking through the churchyard during their summer holiday some time during the 1960s saw a 'funny old lady' dressed in long, dark clothes and a veiled bonnet. When they reached the gate, she was nowhere to be seen and they could not work out where she had gone. When they described her to one of their mothers, she identified her as a lady who had lived at the mill near the church, but who had died twenty years before.

Falmouth Bay, Cornwall

Location: On the south Cornish coast, south of Truro.

Water monsters are sometimes seen in the sea around the British coastline (even sometimes on the beach, as happened at Barmouth in 1975); down the years there have been enough reports of huge unknown creatures from sailors at sea to convince anyone who doubts that there must be many creatures unknown to science still lurking in the vast ocean depths. When these occasionally come to the surface near the shore and are seen, they can create great excitement. During 1975 and 1976 Falmouth Bay seemed to be the regular haunt of a large long-necked creature which was seen by many people, especially during the long hot summer of 1976. Two of the witnesses were fishermen who had seen the creature, nicknamed Morgawr, while they were at sea 25 miles south of Lizard Point. On 9 July 1976 the *Western Morning News* published this report of John Cock and George Vinnicombe's sighting:

> There was visibility for several miles and a flat sea when they had their first sighting. 'It looked like an enormous tyre about 4 feet up in the water with a back like corrugated iron. We came up towards it and must have woken it up because a great head like an enormous seal came out of the water. It just turned its long neck and looked at us and very slowly submerged. The body was black and the head

was grey and we saw a total length of about 22 feet.' Mr Vinnicombe thought it weighed several tons and that if they had not reversed engines they would have been right on top of it. 'It had a big rounded back and there were humps on the top like prehistoric monsters have. We always thought the Loch Ness Monster was a tourist attraction. Now I have my doubts; what we both saw was there.'

George Vinnicombe added: 'Some people think we were nuts but I've been fishing for forty years and have seen nothing like it. I am convinced there is something out there.'

When Morgawr came closer to land, as she often did during those two years, she was on one occasion photographed by a woman who has remained anonymous. Her two photographs show a creature similar to that described by the fishermen. In her judgement the creature seemed to be about 15–18 feet long, and she described it in a letter to the press as follows:

It looked like an elephant waving its trunk, but the trunk was a long neck with a small head on the end, like a snake's head. It had humps on the back which moved in a funny way. The colour was black or very dark brown, and the skin seemed to be like a sealion's . . . the animal frightened me. I would not like to see it any closer. I do not like the way it moved when swimming.

Sighting reports have continued to be published in the press from time to time over the ten years since the major events of the mid-1970s, so it looks as though anyone visiting Falmouth Bay could be lucky enough to see Morgawr.

Haseley church, Warwickshire

Location: The scattered parish of Haseley is 4 miles north-west of Warwick. (SP 234680)

In the 1970s two members of the same family on separate occasions saw a ghost near Haseley church. The son was the first to see it, as he was going home one night on his motorcycle. A woman in a long white dress came out of the churchyard into the road ahead of him, and he had to swerve to avoid her. He thought she was a real person until she disappeared into the hedge on the other side of the road. He has since seen the same ghost twice more, in the same circumstances, and his mother has also seen it. She was walking home alone at dusk when only 15 feet away a figure appeared from the churchyard and crossed

Haseley church.

260

the road, vanishing into the hedge. Few details were noticed, only a woman in a long white robe who moved in a strange way – 'It didn't seem to have any feet' – which might refer to a gliding motion. There may be some connection between the ghost and the former manor house not far away, where a servant was said to have murdered the master of the house in the eighteenth century. The house was also said to have been linked to the church by a secret passage, and perhaps the ghost was following the course of this above-ground.

Irish loughs near Clifden, County Galway

Location: In the far west of Ireland, in Connemara.

This area of western Ireland is studded with lakes of varying sizes, and strange animals have reputedly been seen in a number of them. From time to time Nessie researchers turn their attention to the Irish lakes and follow up some of the more tantalising reports. Loughs Auna and Shanakeever north-east of Clifden, and Lough Nahooin 6 miles away from Shanakeever, are all reputedly monster-haunted.

When the veteran lake monster-hunter Lionel Leslie was in Connemara with some colleagues in 1968, they went to the farm by Lough Nahooin to talk to the owner, Stephen Coyne, who with his wife and children had seen a monster in the lough in February of that year. It was black and had a pole-like head and neck; two humps were seen when it put its head under water, and sometimes a flat tail. The creature was in some ways eel-like, and very flexible judging by its movements. It swam around, and then came closer to the shore, apparently irritated by a barking dog, but retreated when Mr Coyne went to the dog. He had also seen a creature in the lough twenty years before, as wide as a car and with a pale under-belly.

Lough Nahooin being very small, only 100 yards by 80 yards, and averaging 20 feet deep, the researchers decided to net it. The weather was bad, but they struggled with the nets and eventually got them into place. However, they eventually had to leave without having either seen or captured the 'horse-eel', as such creatures are sometimes called, and it seemed difficult to believe that such a tiny lake could hold a 12-foot animal without anyone of their team seeing it during their vigils at the lough.

In 1969 the team came over to Ireland again, and heard of a sighting at Lough Nahooin only a month before, in early September. They spoke to sheep-farmer Thomas Connelly and heard his story. He described seeing a creature bigger than a young donkey, very black in colour, which had four stumpy legs. It was lying in the rushes at first, but then it rolled about and slid into the water where it sank out of sight. This time the researchers decided to drag the lough with chains, but they kept catching on the thick lily beds round the shore. During their investigations they spoke to an old man who had heard his father talk of a monster eel which had become trapped under a bridge by Ballynahinch Castle during a drought. It was about 30 feet long and as thick as a horse. The local men were making a special spear with which to kill it, when a flood came overnight and carried it away to safety. This seems to confirm the idea that lake monsters can and do move around overland, and thus are not confined to the small loughs where they arc sometimes seen. The story also reminds us of the dragons so often dispatched by local heroes in English folklore – or were they not legendary but *real*?

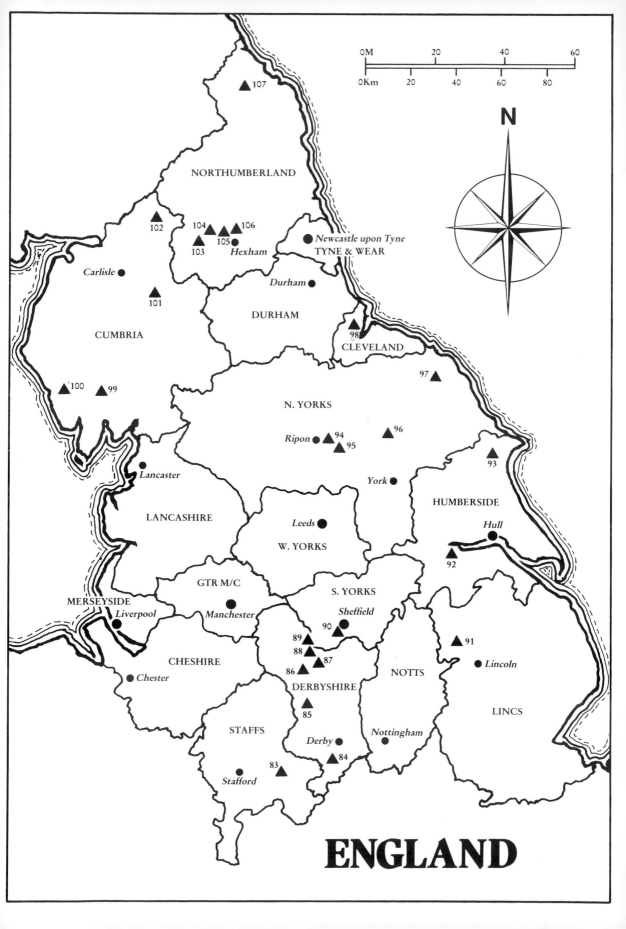

ENGLAND

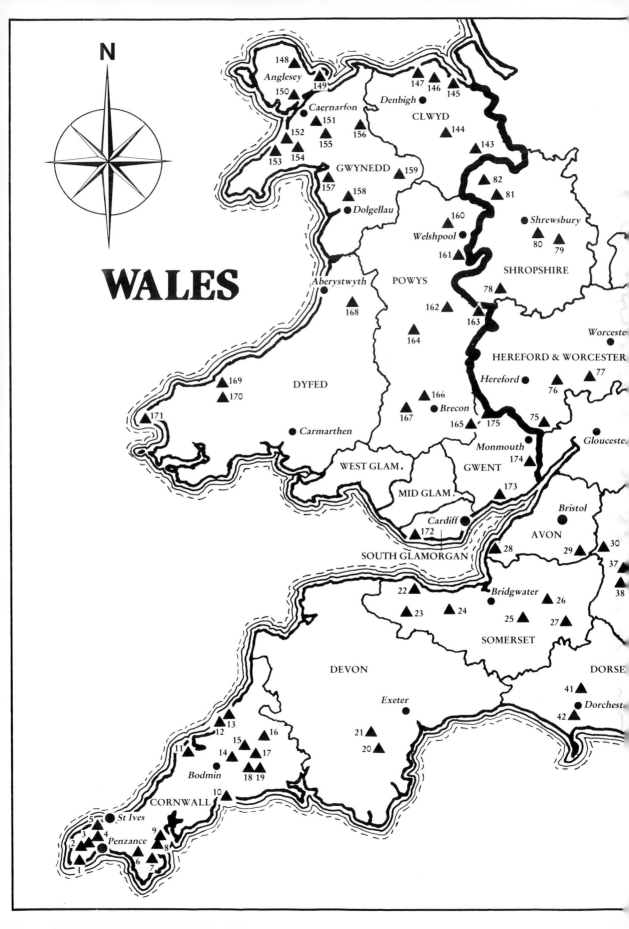

ENGLAND

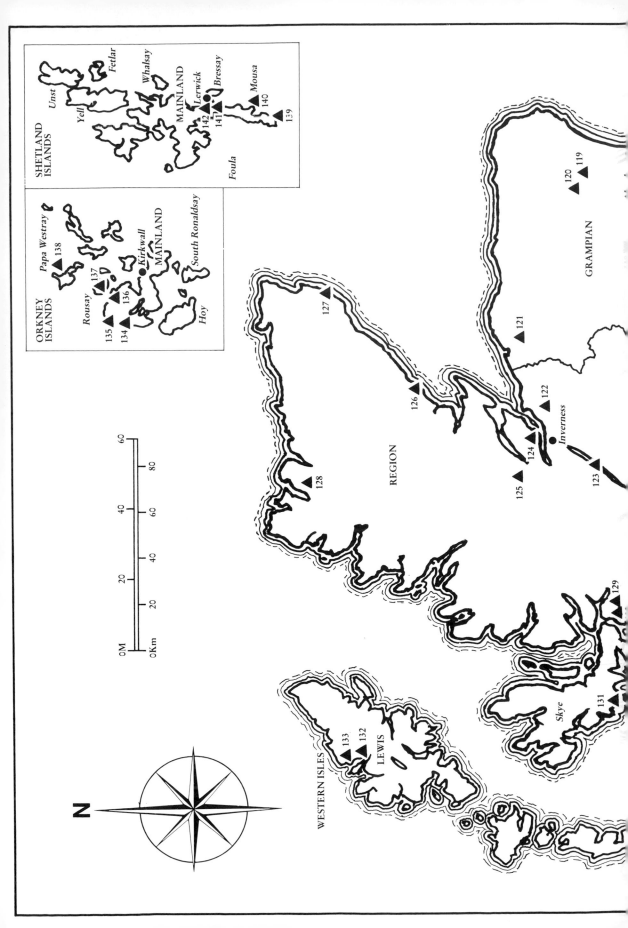

SHETLAND ISLANDS

Unst
Yell
Fetlar
Whalsay
MAINLAND
Lerwick
Bressay
Mousa
142
141
140
139
Foula

ORKNEY ISLANDS

Papa Westray
138
Rousay
137
136
135
134
Kirkwall
MAINLAND
South Ronaldsay
Hoy

WESTERN ISLES
133
132
LEWIS

128

REGION

127

126

125

124

123

122
Inverness

121

GRAMPIAN

120
119

Skye
131

129

N

0M   0   20   40   60
0Km   0   20   40   60   80

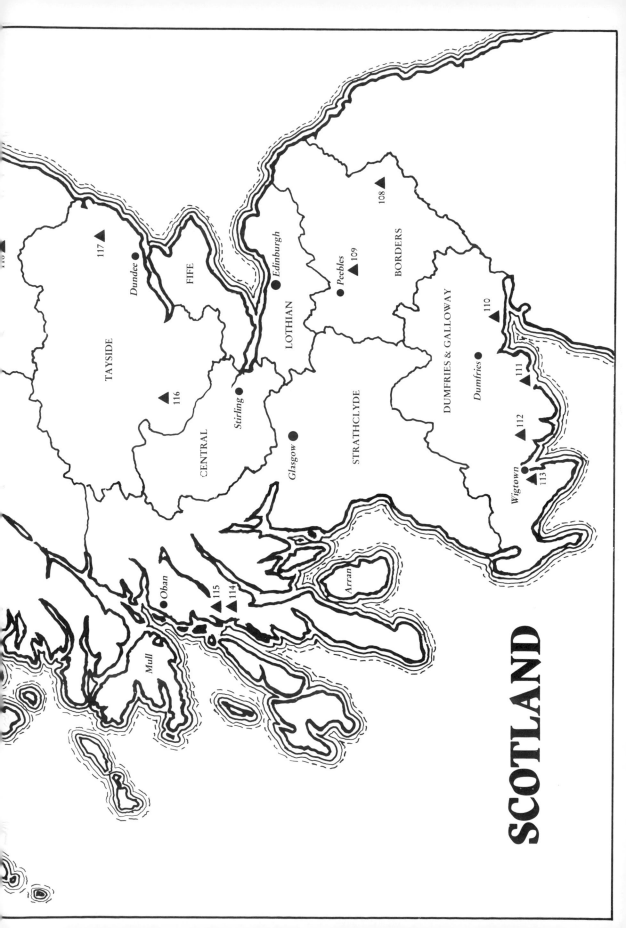

SCOTLAND

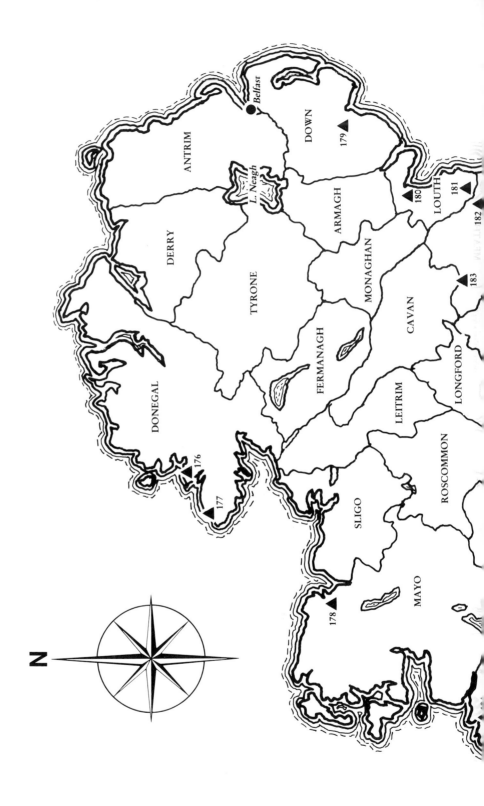

IRELAND

N

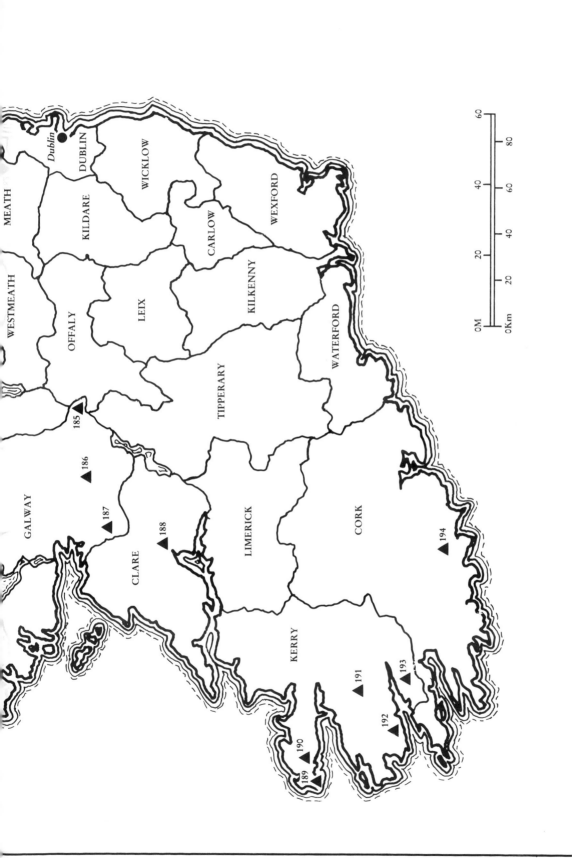

Key to Maps

ENGLAND

Cornwall
1. St Levan Stone (ch. 17)
2. Boscawen-Un stone circle (ch. 1)
3. Carn Euny fogou (ch. 9)
4. Chysauster prehistoric village (ch. 3)
5. Mermaid at Zennor (ch. 17)
6. Helston Furry Dance (ch. 18)
7. Halligye fogou (ch. 9)
8. Hedge maze in Glendurgan Garden (ch. 16)
9. Falmouth Bay (ch. 20)
10. The Tristan Stone (ch. 14)
11. Padstow May Day celebrations (ch. 18)
12. Tintagel Castle (ch. 14)
13. Rocky Valley maze carvings (ch. 16)
14. Cross at Cardinham (ch. 7)
15. Dozmary Pool (ch. 14)
16. Lewannick Ogham stone (ch. 6)
17. The Hurlers stone circles (ch. 1)
18. Holy well at St Cleer (ch. 13)
19. Trethevy Quoit (ch. 2)

Devon
20. Grimspound settlement (ch. 3)
21. The Longstone and stone rows on Shovel Down (ch. 4)

Somerset
22. Minehead Hobby Horse Festival (ch. 18)
23. Caractacus Stone (ch. 17)
24. Carvings in Crowcombe church (chs 11 & 15)

25. Low Ham church (ch. 15)
26. Glastonbury: Abbey, Tor, Chalice Well (ch. 14) and Zodiac (ch. 19)
27. South Cadbury Castle (ch. 14)

Avon
28. Worlebury Camp (ch. 5)
29. Stoney Littleton chambered long barrow (ch. 2)

Wiltshire
30. Saxon chapel at Bradford-on-Avon (ch. 11)
31. Barbury Castle (ch. 5)
32. Avebury henge (ch. 1)
33. Kennet Avenue (ch. 4)
34. Silbury Hill (ch. 8)
35. West Kennet long barrow (ch. 2)
36. Wansdyke (ch. 8)
37. Westbury white horse (ch. 12)
38. Warminster (ch. 20)
39. Stonehenge (ch. 1)
40. Old Sarum ley (ch. 19)

Dorset
41. Cerne Abbas Giant (ch. 12)
42. Maiden Castle (ch. 5)

Hampshire
43. Saxon church at Breamore (ch. 11)
44. Butser Ancient Farm (ch. 3)

East Sussex
45. Lewes Bonfire Night celebrations (ch. 18)
46. Long Man of Wilmington (ch. 12)

Kent
47. Roman pharos at Dover (ch. 10)
48. Richborough Roman fort (ch. 10)

Greater London
49. The King Stone or Coronation Stone, Kingston-upon-Thames (ch. 4)
50. Hampton Court Palace (ch. 20)

Hertfordshire
51. Brent Pelham church (ch. 15)
52. Royston Cave (ch. 9)

Essex
53. Maze tombstone in Hadstock churchyard (ch. 16)
54. Nine Men's Morris, Finchingfield (ch. 16)
55. Site of haunted Borley Rectory (ch. 20)

Suffolk
56. Wissington church (ch. 15)
57. Saxon village, West Stow (ch. 3)
58. Druid Stone, Bungay (ch. 17)

Norfolk
59. Burgh Castle Roman fort (ch. 10)
60. St Withburga's Well, East Dereham (ch. 13)
61. Grimes Graves flint mines (ch. 9)

Cambridgeshire
62. Turf maze at Hilton (ch. 16)

Bedfordshire
63. Holy well at Stevington (ch. 13)

Northamptonshire
64. Saxon church at Brixworth (ch. 11)

Leicestershire
65. Norman church at Tickencote (ch. 11)
66. Roman remains at Leicester (ch. 10)

Warwickshire
67. The Lunt fort (ch. 10)
68. Haseley church (ch. 20)
69. Napton on the Hill church (ch. 20)

Oxfordshire
70. Rollright Stones (ch. 1)
71. St Margaret's Well, Binsey (ch. 13)
72. Uffington church (ch. 15)
73. Uffington white horse and Dragon Hill (ch. 12)
74. Wayland's Smithy chambered long barrow (ch. 2)

Hereford & Worcester
75. King Arthur's Cave (ch. 3)
76. St Edith's Well, Stoke Edith (ch. 13)
77. Herefordshire Beacon hillfort (ch. 5)

Shropshire
78. Arbor Day, Aston-on-Clun (ch. 18)
79. The Wrekin (ch. 17)
80. Wroxeter Roman site (ch. 10)
81. St Winifred's Well, Woolston (ch. 13)
82. Old Oswestry hillfort (ch. 5)

Staffordshire
83. Abbots Bromley Horn Dance (ch. 18)

Derbyshire
84. Repton church crypt (ch. 9)
85. Well-dressing (Tissington indicated) (ch. 18)
86. Arbor Low henge (ch. 1)
87. Nine Stones (ch. 4)
88. Saxon cross at Eyam (ch. 7)
89. Little John's Grave, Hathersage (ch. 17)

South Yorkshire
90. Sword dancing, Sheffield (ch. 18)

Lincolnshire
91. Saxon church at Stow (ch. 11)

Humberside
92. Four mazes at Alkborough (ch. 16)
93. Rudston monolith (ch. 4)

North Yorkshire
94. Sword dancing, Ripon (ch. 18)
95. The Devil's Arrows (ch. 4)
96. Turf maze near Brandsby (ch. 16)
97. Sword dancing, Goathland (ch. 18)

274

275

Bibliography

Alcock, Leslie, *Arthur's Britain: History and Archaeology AD 367–634*, Allen Lane, 1971; Pelican Books, 1973

Alexander, Marc, *British Folklore, Myths and Legends*, Weidenfeld & Nicolson, 1982

Ashe, Geoffrey, *Camelot and the Vision of Albion*, William Heinemann, 1975

—— *A Guidebook to Arthurian Britain*, Longman Group, 1980; Aquarian Press/Thorsons Publishers, 1983

Barnatt, John, *Stone Circles of the Peak*, Turnstone Books, 1978

Bowen, E.G., *Saints, Seaways and Settlements in the Celtic Lands*, University of Wales Press, 1977

Bord, Janet and Colin, *Mysterious Britain*, Garnstone Press, 1972; Paladin/Granada Publishing, 1974

—— *The Secret Country: An Interpretation of the Folklore of Ancient Sites in the British Isles*, Paul Elek, 1976; Paladin/Granada Publishing, 1978

—— *A Guide to Ancient Sites in Britain*, Latimer New Dimensions, 1978; Paladin/Granada Publishing, 1979

—— *Alien Animals*, Paul Elek/Granada Publishing, 1980; Panther/Granada Publishing, 1985

—— *Bigfoot Casebook*, Granada Publishing, 1982

—— *Earth Rites: Fertility Practices in Pre-Industrial Britain*, Granada Publishing, 1982; Paladin/Granada Publishing, 1983

—— *The Evidence for Bigfoot and Other Man-Beasts*, Aquarian Press/Thorsons Publishers, 1984

—— *Sacred Waters: Holy Wells and Water Lore in Britain and Ireland*, Granada Publishing, 1985

—— *Modern British Mysteries: 100 Years of Strange Events*, Grafton Books, forthcoming (probably 1987)

Bord, Janet, *Mazes and Labyrinths of the World*, Latimer New Dimensions, 1976

Brennan, Martin, *The Boyne Valley Vision*, The Dolmen Press, 1980

—— *The Stars and the Stones*, Thames & Hudson, 1983

Burke, John, *Roman England*, Weidenfeld & Nicolson, 1983

Burl, Aubrey, *The Stone Circles of the British Isles*, Yale University Press, 1976

—— *Prehistoric Avebury*, Yale University Press, 1979

—— *Rites of the Gods*, J. M. Dent & Sons, 1981

Butler, Brenda, Dot Street and Jenny Randles, Sky Crash: A Cosmic Conspiracy, Neville Spearman, 1984

Castleden, Rodney, *The Wilmington Giant: The Quest for a Lost Myth*, Turnstone Press, 1983

Cavendish, Richard, *King Arthur and the Grail: The Arthurian Legends and Their Meaning*, Weidenfeld & Nicolson, 1978

—— *Prehistoric England*, Weidenfeld & Nicolson, 1983

Chippendale, Christopher, *Stonehenge Complete*, Thames & Hudson, 1983

Coate, Randoll and Adrian Fisher, *A Celebration of Mazes*, Minotaur Designs (40 Whitecroft, St Albans, Herts), 1982

Dames, Michael, *The Silbury Treasure: The Great Goddess Rediscovered*, Thames & Hudson, 1976

—— *The Avebury Cycle*, Thames & Hudson, 1977

Devereux, Paul and Ian Thomson, *The Ley Hunter's Companion: Aligned Ancient Sites: A New Study with Field Guide and Maps*, Thames & Hudson, 1979

Devereux, Paul, *Earth Lights: Towards an Understanding of the UFO Enigma*, Turnstone Press, 1982

Dinsdale, Tim, *Loch Ness Monster*, Routledge & Kegan Paul, 4th edn 1982

Dyer, James, *Southern England: An Archaeological Guide*, Faber & Faber, 1973

—— *The Penguin Guide to Prehistoric England and Wales*, Allen Lane, 1981; Penguin Books, 1982

Ellis, Peter Berresford, *Celtic Inheritance*, Muller, Blond & White, 1985

Evans, Hilary, *The Evidence for UFOs*, Aquarian Press, 1983

—— *Visions, Apparitions, Alien Visitors: A Comparative Study of the Entity Enigma*, Aquarian Press, 1984

Francis, Di, *Cat Country: The Quest for the British Big Cat*, David & Charles, 1983

Gauld, Alan and A. D. Cornell, *Poltergeists*, Routledge & Kegan Paul, 1979

Glob, P. V., *The Bog People*, Faber & Faber, 1969; Paladin/Granada Publishing, 1971

Bibliography

Graves, Tom, *Needles of Stone*, Turnstone Press, 1978; Panther/Granada Publishing, 1980

Grinsell, Leslie V., *Barrow, Pyramid and Tomb: Ancient Burial Customs in Egypt, the Mediterranean and the British Isles*, Thames & Hudson, 1975

—— *Folklore of Prehistoric Sites in Britain*, David & Charles, 1976

Hadingham, Evan, *Ancient Carvings in Britain*, Garnstone Press, 1974

—— *Early Man and the Cosmos*, William Heinemann, 1983

Harbison, Peter, *Guide to the National Monuments in the Republic of Ireland*, Gill & Macmillan, 1975

Hogg, A. H. A., *Hill-Forts of Britain*, Paladin/Granada Publishing, 1984

Hole, Christina, *English Traditional Customs*, B. T. Batsford, 1975

—— *British Folk Customs*, Hutchinson Publishing, 1976

Houlder, Christopher, *Wales: An Archaeological Guide*, Faber & Faber, 1974

Howard, Michael A., *The Runes and Other Magical Alphabets*, Thorsons Publishers, 1978

Jackson, Anthony, *The Symbol Stones of Scotland*, Orkney Press, 1984

Johnson, Stephen, *Later Roman Britain*, Routledge & Kegan Paul, 1980; Paladin/Granada Publishing, 1982

Jones, Lawrence E., *The Beauty of English Churches*, Constable, 1978

Kerr, Nigel and Mary, *A Guide to Anglo-Saxon Sites*, Granada Publishing, and Paladin, 1982

—— *A Guide to Norman Sites in Britain*, Granada Publishing, 1984; Paladin/Granada Publishing, 1985

Kightly, Charles, *Folk Heroes of Britain*, Thames & Hudson, 1982

Krupp, E. C. (ed.), *In Search of Ancient Astronomies*, Chatto & Windus, 1980; Penguin Books, 1984

Laing, Lloyd, *Celtic Britain*, Routledge & Kegan Paul, 1979; Paladin/Granada Publishing, 1981

Laing, Lloyd and Jennifer, *Anglo-Saxon England*, Routledge & Kegan Paul, 1979; Paladin/Granada Publishing, 1982

—— *A Guide to the Dark Age Remains in Britain*, Constable, 1979

—— *The Origins of Britain*, Routledge & Kegan Paul, 1980; Paladin/Granada Publishing, 1982

Legg, Rodney, *Romans in Britain*, William Heinemann, 1983

278

Logan, Patrick, *The Holy Wells of Ireland*, Colin Smythe, 1980

MacKenzie, Andrew, *Hauntings and Apparitions*, William Heinemann, 1982; Paladin/Granada Publishing, 1983

MacKie, Euan W., *Scotland: An Archaeological Guide*, Faber & Faber, 1975

—— *Science and Society in Prehistoric Britain*, Elek Books, 1977

McMann, Jean, *Riddles of the Stone Age: Rock Carvings of Ancient Europe*, Thames & Hudson, 1980

Marples, Morris, *White Horses and Other Hill Figures*, Country Life, 1949; S.R. Publishers, 1970; Alan Sutton Publishing, 1981

Matthews, W. H., *Mazes and Labyrinths: Their History and Development*, Longmans, Green, 1922; Dover Publications, 1970

Michell, John, *The Old Stones of Land's End*, Garnstone Press, 1974

—— *The Earth Spirit: Its Ways, Shrines and Mysteries*, Thames & Hudson, 1975

—— *A Little History of Astro-Archaeology: Stages in the Transformation of a Heresy*, Thames & Hudson, 1977

—— *Megalithomania: Artists, Antiquarians and Archaeologists at the Old Stone Monuments*, Thames & Hudson, 1982

—— *The New View Over Atlantis* (fully revised edition of *The View Over Atlantis*, first published 1969), Thames & Hudson, 1983

Michell, John and Robert J. M. Rickard, *Phenomena: A Book of Wonders*, Thames & Hudson, 1977

—— *Living Wonders: Mysteries and Curiosities of the Animal World*, Thames & Hudson, 1982

Morris, Ronald W. B., *The Prehistoric Rock Art of Argyll*, Dolphin Press, 1977

—— *The Prehistoric Rock Art of Galloway and the Isle of Man*, Blandford Press, 1979

Morris, Ruth and Frank, *Scottish Healing Wells*, The Alethea Press (Everton, Sandy, Beds), 1981

Muir, Richard, *Reading the Celtic Landscapes*, Michael Joseph, 1985

O'Kelly, Michael J., *Newgrange: Archaeology, Art and Legend*, Thames & Hudson, 1982

Owen, Gale R., *Rites and Religions of the Anglo-Saxons*, David & Charles, 1981

Page, R. I., *An Introduction to English Runes*, Methuen, 1973

Bibliography

Pegg, Bob, *Rites and Riots: Folk Customs of Britain and Europe*, Blandford Press, 1981

Pennick, Nigel, *The Ancient Science of Geomancy: Man in Harmony with the Earth*, Thames & Hudson, 1979

—— *The Subterranean Kingdom: A Survey of Man-Made Structures Beneath the Earth*, Turnstone Press, 1983

Piggott, Stuart, *The Druids*, Thames & Hudson paperback, 1985

Randles, Jenny, *The Pennine UFO Mystery*, Granada Publishing, 1983

—— *UFO Reality: A Critical Look at the Physical Evidence*, Robert Hale, 1983

Reynolds, Peter J., *Iron-Age Farm: The Butser Experiment*, Colonnade Books/British Museum Publications, 1979

Rickard, Robert and Richard Kelly, *Photographs of the Unknown*, New English Library, 1980

Ritchie, Graham and Anna, *Scotland: Archaeology and Early History*, Thames & Hudson paperback, 1985

Robins, Don, *Circles of Silence*, Souvenir Press, 1985

Rodwell, Warwick and James Bentley, *Our Christian Heritage*, Guild Publishing/Book Club Associates, 1984

Ross, Anne, *Pagan Celtic Britain: Studies in Iconography and Tradition*, Routledge & Kegan Paul, 1967; Cardinal/Sphere Books, 1974

Rutherford, Ward, *The Druids: Magicians of the West*, Aquarian Press, 1983

Saward, Jeff, *The Book of British Troy Towns*, Caerdroia Project (53 Thundersley Grove, Thundersley, Benfleet, Essex), 1982 (also publishes a regular magazine on mazes)

Screeton, Paul, *Quicksilver Heritage: The Mystic Leys: Their Legacy of Ancient Wisdom*, Thorsons Publishers, 1974

Senior, Michael, *Myths of Britain*, Guild Publishing/Book Club Associates, 1979

Simpson, Jacqueline, *British Dragons*, B. T. Batsford, 1980

Streit, Jakob, *Sun and Cross: The Development from Megalithic Culture to Early Christianity in Ireland*, Floris Books, 1984

Taylor, Christopher and Richard Muir, *Visions of the Past*, J. M. Dent, 1983

Thomas, Charles, *Celtic Britain*, Thames & Hudson, 1985

Wacher, John, *The Coming of Rome*, Routledge & Kegan Paul, 1979; Paladin/Granada Publishing, 1981

Wainwright, Richard, *A Guide to the Prehistoric Remains in Britain*, Volume One: *South and East*, Constable, 1978

Watkins, Alfred, *The Old Straight Track*, Methuen, 1925; Garnstone Press, 1970

—— *The Ley Hunter's Manual: A Guide to Early Tracks*, first published 1927; Turnstone Press, 1983

Weir, Anthony, *Early Ireland: A Field Guide*, Blackstaff Press, 1980

Westwood, Jennifer, *Albion: A Guide to Legendary Britain*, Granada Publishing, 1985

Whitlock, Ralph, *Here Be Dragons*, George Allen & Unwin, 1983

Williamson, Tom and Liz Bellamy, *Ley Lines in Question*, World's Work, 1983

Wilson, Roger J. A., *A Guide to the Roman Remains in Britain*, Constable, 1975, 2nd edn 1980

Witchell, Nicholas, *The Loch Ness Story*, Terence Dalton, 1974; Corgi, 1982

Index

282